COMPLETE BOOK OF
HOME STORAGE OF VEGETABLES AND FRUITS

COMPLETE BOOK OF

HOME STORAGE

OF

VEGETABLES

AND

FRUITS

EVELYN V. LOVEDAY

ILLUSTRATED BY DOUGLAS MERRILEES

GARDEN WAY PUBLISHING CO., CHARLOTTE, VERMONT

Standard Book Number: 0-88266-002-0
Library of Congress Catalog Card Number: 72-80390

GARDEN WAY PUBLISHING CO., CHARLOTTE, VERMONT 05445

PRINTED IN THE UNITED STATES

CONTENTS

PREFACE   vii
1 STORAGE METHODS   1
2 COMMON STORAGE   7
3 DRYING   32
4 CURING AND SALTING   52
5 CANNING   61
6 FREEZERS AND FREEZING TIPS   89
7 FREEZING VEGETABLES AND FRUITS   108
8 RECIPES   136
   BIBLIOGRAPHY   149
   INDEX   151

ILLUSTRATIONS

1 OUTDOOR MOUND   12

2 BARREL STORAGE   13

3 PIT   14

4 CELERY STORAGE   17

5 CELERY AND CHINESE CABBAGE STORAGE   18

6 CABBAGE STORAGE   19

7 CABBAGE STORAGE   19

8 BASEMENT STORAGE ROOM   24

9 SOLAR DRIER   40

10 OVEN DRIER   41

11 ON-STOVE DRIER   42

12 STAND TO CONVERT ON-STOVE DRIER   43

13 ELECTRIC DRIER   44

14 PAPER BAG HERB DRYING   49

15 KRAUT CUTTING BOARD   54

16 STEAM-PRESSURE CANNER   63

17 JAR LIDS   65

18 WATER-BATH CANNER   66

19 CHEST FREEZER   91

20 UPRIGHT FREEZER   93

PREFACE

What methods of storage of your vegetables and fruits will best meet your needs? Will it be canning, drying or freezing? Or will you build a root cellar and an outdoor storage mound?

Whatever your preferences are in methods of storage, this book will be your guide for bringing your surplus produce from the garden and orchard to your winter table.

The Complete Book of Home Storage of Vegetables and Fruits has been written to take you step by step through each known method of storage. The text is complete with many useful charts, tables and excellent illustrations.

You will not be surprised to learn that an author of a reference book like this one does not take all the information out of his own experience. I have talked with many old-time gardeners, corresponded with several authorities and read a great deal, too. I wanted to give you as much information as possible and found it scattered around in many places. The bibliography includes material which I found helpful.

I bow thankfully in the direction of the many individuals who gave me suggestions out of their own wisdom and experience. This shared knowledge about storage methods has enabled me to relate accurate, "tried and true" information.

It is my hope that you will let this book guide you to the storage methods that meet your own special needs and available facilities. It will be work, but also, adventurous fun.

Anyway, have at it, and happy winter eating!

EVELYN V. LOVEDAY
May 1, 1972

"Let us grasp the situation,
Solve the complicated plot. . ."
THE GONDOLIERS[1]

One
STORAGE METHODS

How will you decide which method, or combination of methods, will best meet the needs of your family? Many factors will influence your decision, but the most important ones are the facilities you have available (or decide to buy or build), the climate in which you live, and your family's likes and dislikes.

Don't underestimate the latter. A row of jars of ruby-red beets is a beautiful sight, but if no one in your family will eat a beet except under protest, your time and energy have been wasted.

As to climate, practically no one in Chicago wears shorts in winter. If you live in a climate where the temperatures are seldom below freezing you will have difficulty with outdoor common storage, but then, you are probably having fresh lettuce most of the year 'round.

What are the known methods of vegetable and fruit storage? There are five: common storage, drying, curing, and salting, canning, and freezing. Table 1 gives you a quick glance at methods which can be used for specific vegetables and fruits.

Following the table is a brief overview of the five storage methods. This is to introduce you to the basic concepts involved in each method before proceeding to the more detailed discussions in the following chapters.

DISCUSSION OF METHODS

COMMON STORAGE Certain fruits and vegetables having slow life processes can be stored successfully in winter in cold, dark places. This is an inexpensive way to keep root and some other vegetables, as well as apples and pears. There are several forms of outdoor and indoor

---

1. Introductory quotations to all the chapters are from the works of Gilbert and Sullivan.

TABLE 1
VEGETABLE STORAGE

Vegetable	Common Storage	Drying	Curing & Salting	Canning	Freezing
Artichokes					X
Asparagus		X		X	X
Beans (all kinds)		X	X	X	X
Beets	X	X	X	X	X
Broccoli		X		X	X
Brussels Sprouts				X	X
Cabbage	X	X	X	X	X
Carrots	X	X		X	X
Cauliflower			X	X	X
Celery	X	X		X (cooked)	X (cooked)
Corn		X		X	X
Endive	X				
Greens (all kinds)		X		X	X
Herbs		X			X
Kale		X	X	X	X
Mushrooms		X		X	X
Okra		X		X	X
Onions	X	X		X	
Parsnips	X	X	X	X	X
Peas		X (mature)		X	X
Peppers	X	X		X	X
Potatoes (white)	X			X	X
Potatoes (sweet)	X	X		X	X
Pumpkins	X	X		X	X
Rutabagas	X	X	X	X	X
Salsify	X				
Squash	X	X		X	X
Tomatoes	X	X (paste)	X (green)	X	X
Turnips	X	X	X	X	X

FRUIT AND BERRY STORAGE

Apples	X	X		X	X
Apricots		X		X	X
Berries		X		X	X
Cherries		X		X	X
Cranberries				X	X
Figs		X		X	
Fruit Juices				X	X
Grapefruit				X	X
Peaches		X		X	X
Pears	X	X		X	X
Plums		X		X	

common storage and they are fully described in the chapter on the subject.

Almost all nutritive values are well-retained in common storage except vitamin C which is gradually lost. For instance, one study showed that potatoes, in the period from January to April lost half of their vitamin C. The loss of this vitamin in stored root vegetables in the late winter and early spring months means that special effort must be made to obtain it from other foods: i.e. canned tomatoes, citrus fruits and fresh vegetables such as kale, broccoli and cabbage.

DRYING This method of storing vegetables and fruits is less popular currently than some other methods, perhaps because too little is known about it. Not all produce is satisfactory to the taste after drying and some experimentation on the part of the homemaker may be necessary, if she is to please the family.

Dried apples, dried corn, beans and herbs are types of home-dried foods that have always been well liked.

The principle behind the drying method of preservation is that spoilage organisms cannot grow without considerable moisture. After drying, the food must be stored in airtight containers in a cool, dry place.

A and B vitamins in dried foods are comparatively stable, but as a rule most of the vitamin C is lost. Nutrients other than vitamins are not affected. Still, there are some losses if the soaking water (freshening process) is thrown away, or if each step in the drying process is not carefully followed.

Those who prefer natural foods with no additives will question the recommendation made for the addition of sulfur. Sulfur is used with light-colored fruit to prevent it from darkening; also, it helps the product to retain the vitamins A and C. However, it is not absolutely necessary and this will be discussed further in the chapter on drying.

In some sections of the country there is sunshine enough to dry food outdoors, but in most localities it is better to use artificial heat; then the temperature can be controlled, as well as the humidity and ventilation. Under these controlled conditions, the process is often called dehydration, but drying is a good name for the method used at home.

Drying is a longish process, whether by sun or artificial heat, and one must be prepared to stay with it as a clock-watcher for 10-12 hours, per procedure. If you're the restless type, this is the day you can get some knitting or reading done, while keeping one eye on the clock.

CURING AND SALTING Perhaps one of the oldest methods of preserving food is with salt. If large amounts of salt are used, the growth of spoilage agents is inhibited. This method results in very salty products that must be freshened and when this is done some of the nutrients may be dissolved and lost.

With only small amounts of salt, fermentation occurs. Bacteria change the sugars of the vegetable to lactic acid, and the acid with the salt prevents the growth of spoilage organisms. Lactic acid fermentation is the method used in making sauerkraut, dill pickles, green tomatoes and other fermented vegetables such as sauer beans, turnip kraut and cauliflower.

This method of salting in weak brine yields vegetables that are attractive in appearance and crisp in texture. Since they do not need to be soaked in fresh water to remove excess salt, they retain fair amounts of nutrients. They have a pleasing acid, slightly salty flavor.

CANNING Foods preserved by this well-known standard method retain their values well. Fruits, fruit juices and tomatoes retain more vitamin C than do non-acid vegetables. It is important that all the juices of vegetables and fruits be used in heating and serving canned foods because they contain dissolved minerals, protein and sugar, as well as 30-50 per cent of the vitamins. Vitamins in canned foods tend to decrease during storage.

There are different methods of canning which are discussed in the chapter on this subject, but nothing in canning is more important than following directions exactly. This is the only method of home storage of vegetables from which one can get botulism poisoning, which can be avoided by correct processing. This is discussed in detail in Chapter five.

Canning equipment involves some financial outlay (not nearly as much as a freezer), but like the freezer lasts many years and thus is amortized over a long period of time.

FREEZING No book on the storage of produce would be complete without a discussion of freezing, for it is one of the simplest, easiest ways in which to preserve food. Moreover, foods properly prepared and quickly frozen retain high amounts of all nutrients and are most similar in all ways to fresh foods.

While the financial outlay for a freezer is considerable, one of reputable make should last for many years so that the cost is amortized over a long time.

Current running expenses for packaging materials can be kept to a minimum by using one's ingenuity. However, proper (entire) packaging is very important.

If you live in an area where there are frequent and protracted power failures, it would be advisable to locate a convenient source of supply for dry ice which will hold your freezer at proper temperature. At any rate, do protect your frozen things with an alternate method of keeping them frozen. Could anything be sadder than losing an entire freezer-full of food because it's all thawed?

This is probably as good a time as any to tell you that despite the miracle of the freezer there are some vegetables that you just can't freeze successfully. In general, these are those which you serve raw and crisp for salads, such as lettuce, cucumbers, onions, celery and radishes.

SOME GENERAL RULES FOR STORAGE

Before discussing the particulars of each method of storage as I do in the following chapters, there are some general rules for preservation which cannot be over-emphasized. In fact, you will find them repeated often in this book, not because I want to bore you, but because I want to make an insistent demand on your attention. I don't want you to find decayed produce in your common storage, to be ill from improperly canned foods, or to dislike the flavor of what you worked so hard to store. Here we go!

1. Use fresh products picked in their prime. (There are a few exceptions to this which will be noted later.)

2. For freezing, canning, or drying, preserve the foods immediately after picking before they lose their quality and vitamins. Follow the particular rules for each process carefully.

3. Store all canned, dried, or raw produce in a cool, dry place.

4. Vegetables and fruits that are to be stored raw must be absolutely free of all decay or cuts. Handle your products as though they were eggs in order not to bruise them. The old saying that one rotten apple can spoil a barrel full is very literally true.

5. All produce stored by any method discussed in this book should be eaten within a year. Yes, I know of people as do you who eat frozen or canned vegetables and fruits much older than that. But I'm going to stick with the nutrition experts on this point and insist that you store only what can be consumed by your family by the time next season's garden is producing. You will be far better nourished if you follow this plan.

Now you know something in general about the five storage methods and a few guidelines which apply to those methods.

Let's explore the particulars of each method in detail in the following chapters, so that you can decide how best to provide appetizing, nutritious vegetables and fruits for your family throughout the winter.

Carry on!

"Quiet calm deliberation
Disentangles every knot."
THE GONDOLIERS

Two
COMMON STORAGE

Our ancestors usually had no furnaces in their cellars—in fact, the cellars generally had dirt floors and were chilly and damp. So, they easily had root cellars in which their root vegetables were stored for the winter months. Now, most of our houses must have special facilities built for cold storage unless, as is often possible, the outdoors is used.

We will be taking a close look at the many forms of common storage: outdoor pits and mounds; barrels buried in straw; vegetables left in the ground, well-mulched with hay, straw or leaves; barrels or boxes in the garage with vegetables buried in sand or sawdust; cellar storage rooms; and even a sauna.

Your choice of a storage space will depend, of course, on the climate in which you live and the facilities at hand. In very cold sections, for example, extra precautions against freezing have to be taken. In warm climates the problem is to keep temperatures low enough to prevent decay from starting. In excessively dry areas it may be necessary to increase the moisture in the air of a storage compartment. In humid localities some method must be employed to eliminate excessive moisture.

Because of all these variables I cannot give you a set of step-by-step rules such as I am able to give you for other storage methods.

The best I can do is chart out a general course for you. You can fill out the specifics by getting advice from your neighbors experienced in common storage. Another good source of information will be your county agent and the Extension Service of your state agricultural college. Don't hestitate to call on them for help. Your taxes are helping to pay for this service, and their advice will be geared to your local conditions.

Vegetables and fruits which lend themselves well to common storage are potatoes, carrots, beets, turnips, cabbage, squash, pumpkins, celery, salsify, parsnips, winter pears and some varieties of apples. Specifics for each will be found later in this chapter.

The reader needs a careful warning here: i.e., unlike standard canning methods, for example, there is not total agreement among authorities about some aspects of common storage. Some authorities would have you carefully wash each vegetable or fruit before storing it. Others say that washing is unnecessary and that you must always use sawdust—never sand—for packing in boxes or barrels. And so it goes.

We, at Garden Way Research, decided that there is no one "absolutely correct" way for all climates and all people. Thus, I am presenting all of the many ideas we have experienced, or read about, and the choice is up to you. You will decide what seems most practical for you in terms of facilities, space and climate. No doubt you will experiment with more than one kind of common storage, particularly if you are relatively new at this game. I do vouch for the fact that everything suggested here has been solidly recommended by experienced authorities.

There are some particular items of advice which apply to all forms of common storage. They are:

1. Vegetables for common storage are best when planted late; just in time to get ripe but not too ripe, before frost.

2. Harvesting, in most cases, (exceptions are noted later) should be delayed as long as possible without danger of freezing. Several root crops can withstand some freezing without damage, but not alternate thawing and freezing.

3. All vegetables and fruits to be stored should be handled with great care to avoid bruises and cuts.

4. Never store root crops immediately after harvesting, as they retain "field heat" for several hours. Also, they must be as dry as possible. Try to choose a sunny, dry day (not right after a rain) for harvesting; then, allow the crops to remain on the ground at least throughout the night to cool. Potatoes are an exception to this: they need

only a few hours' drying. Onions should dry outdoors for about a week.

5. Store only produce of good quality. Diseased or blemished vegetables and fruits may be used early in the fall, or preserved in some other way.

6. Proper storage temperature is a most important factor. With few exceptions (noted later), the most desirable temperature is close to 32°F. and except for potatoes, vegetables are not injured at this temperature. However, to avoid freezing, it is best to shoot for a temperature between 35°-40° F. whether in outdoor or indoor storage.

6. Proper humidity levels and ventilation are also factors in successful storage. For information on temperature and humidity see Table 2.

7. When preparing any vegetable for common storage, do leave an inch or so of tops or stems on. If you don't, the crop will "bleed" (you can see this in beets—others don't show it), and nutrients will be lost. Also, leaving a little top on prevents scars in which decay can start.

8. In all forms of common storage, with the exception of potatoes, onions, apples and pears, the units of produce should be hung or packed in such manner so as not to touch each other directly. This will prevent spread of decay.

HOW LONG? WHO KNOWS? Trying to predict how long your stored produce will remain in good condition is in the same class with trying to predict the weather. Everything depends on your climate, the care with which you prepared your storage area, and the condition of the products when stored. Table 2 should be consulted as a guideline only, not for hard-and-fast information.

CLEANING AND PACKING As we said earlier, there are many different opinions (some outright contradictory) about common storage; and one point of difference is on the subject of washing, or brushing crops before storage. Some believe the crops must be washed or brushed off with care, while other authorities believe that this is a great error and that produce should be handled as little as possible to prevent decay. This latter opinion seems more logical but if you're compulsively neat and want to wash your produce prior to storing, you have some authori-

TABLE 2

FREEZING POINTS, RECOMMENDED STORAGE CONDITIONS, AND LENGTH OF STORAGE PERIOD OF VEGETABLES AND FRUITS

Commodity	Freezing Point °F.	Place to Store	Storage Conditions Temperature °F.	Storage Conditions Humidity	Length of Storage Period
Vegetables:					
Dry beans and peas		Any cool, dry place	32° to 40°	Dry	As long as desired.
Late cabbage	30.4	Pit, trench, or outdoor cellar	Near 32° as possible	Moderately moist.	Through late fall and winter.
Cauliflower	30.3	Storage cellar	Same as above.	Same as above.	6 to 8 weeks.
Late celery	31.6	Pit or trench; roots in soil in storage cellar.	Same as above.	Same as above.	Through late fall and winter.
Endive	31.9	Roots in soil in storage cellar	Same as above.	Same as above.	2 to 3 months.
Onions	30.6	Any cool, dry place	Same as above.	Dry	Through fall and winter.
Parsnips	30.4	Where they grew, or in storage cellar.	Same as above.	Moist	Same as above.
Peppers	30.7	Unheated basement or room	45° to 50°	Moderately moist.	2 to 3 weeks.
Potatoes	30.9	Pit or in storage cellar	35° to 40°	Same as above.	Through fall and winter.
Pumpkins and squashes	30.5	Home cellar or basement	55°	Moderately dry.	Same as above.
Root crops (miscellaneous).		Pit or in storage cellar	Near 32° as possible	Moist	Same as above.
Sweet potatoes	29.7	Home cellar or basement	55° to 60°	Moderately dry.	Same as above.
Tomatoes (mature green).	31.0	Same as above.	55° to 70°	Same as above.	4 to 6 weeks.
Fruits:					
Apples	29.0	Fruit storage cellar	Near 32° as possible	Moderately moist.	Through fall and winter.
Grapefruit	29.8	Same as above.	Same as above.	Same as above.	4 to 6 weeks.
Grapes	28.1	Same as above.	Same as above.	Same as above.	1 to 2 months.
Oranges	30.5	Same as above.	Same as above.	Same as above.	4 to 6 weeks.
Pears	29.2	Same as above.	Same as above.	Same as above.	4 to 6 weeks.

ties to back you up in your choice. However, do be sure
it's all thoroughly dry when stored.

Then you can get any number of authorities to sub-
stantiate your choice of packing material, be it dry sand,
damp sand, dry sawdust or leaves.

The proponents of sawdust will argue that it keeps
produce dormant; that sand (damp or dry) imparts an
unpleasant flavor to vegetables and fruits; and, also that
sawdust is an excellent insulator, thus protecting the produce from drying out, or from getting too warm. They used
to use sawdust in the old ice houses as an insulator, didn't
they?

A lumber mill dispensing free sawdust may not be convenient to your location, so you may want to use sand.
If it is damp, and kept damp, your produce may not remain dormant, but will continue to grow too large for good
taste. However, it won't shrivel.

Dry sand or leaves will be fine, except for those vegetables which tend to shrivel. Then a source of humidity
must be used, no matter how simple. This is discussed at
length in the section on indoor storage.

You can see that much of the "how-to" is up to you; you
choose a method, or combination of methods, and try it.
Next year, your own experience in your specific climate
and facilities, as well as your taste buds, will tell you what
method was best for you. I just mention procedures which
have worked for others.

Regardless of what packing material you use, it can be
put into your compost heap, or spread in your garden
when you're through with it. In fact, it should not be re-
used for packing away produce the second year. More
to come about cleanliness in storage later in this chapter.

OUTDOOR STORAGE IN MOUNDS, PITS, BARRELS, TILES, CARTONS AND THE GROUND

These very cheap and quite simple methods of common
storage are useful for winter apples and pears as well as
for root crops, celery and cabbage. However, they should
not be attempted unless you live in a climate where the
outdoor temperatures in winter average 30°F. or below.

Also, if you live in an area where the snow can be four to six feet deep (as it is here at Garden Way), you want to remember that shovelling snow will be necessary in order to get at your produce. Maybe you're young and think snow shovelling is fun. In that case, don't let me deter you!

MOUNDS A cone-shaped mound (see Fig. 1) may be built on the ground in a well-drained location.

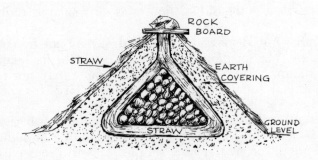

FIGURE 1   OUTDOOR MOUND

Build the mound as follows:

Spread a layer of straw, leaves, or other bedding on the ground. Over this spread a generous length of hardware cloth (unless you want to feed the rodents instead of your family).

Stack the vegetables or fruits on the hardware cloth in a cone-shaped pile. Do not store vegetables and fruits together.

Cover the pile with more bedding and pack it well.

Cover the entire pile with three or four inches of soil.

Firm the soil with the back of a shovel to make the mound waterproof.

Cover all with six to eight inches of straw or hay to keep the soil from freezing too hard.

Small mounds containing only a few bushels of vegetables or fruits will get sufficient ventilation if you let the bedding material over the produce extend through the soil at the top of the pile as shown in Fig. 1. Cover the top of the pile with a board, or piece of sheet metal to protect the stored products from rain; a stone will hold the cover in place.

To ventilate a large mound, place two or three stakes up through the center of the pile to form a flue. Cap the flue with two pieces of board nailed together to form a cross.

It is difficult to remove produce from these mounds in cold weather; and once the mound is opened, the entire contents will have to be removed, probably, since if the earth covering is frozen it cannot be replaced on the mound successfully. Hence, it is better to have several small mounds rather than one large one. Then you need open only one at a time to get a variety of produce. When a variety of vegetables or fruits is stored in the same mound, separate the varieties with straw or leaves.

When vegetables and fruits are brought into the house from outdoor storage they should first be inspected for decay. Cut out any blemished areas from the produce and use that product first. The rest should be put in plastic bags and stored in the refrigerator or a chilly area of the house until required for use.

One simple type of pit is shown in Fig. 2, which is only a barrel covered with several layers of straw and earth.

FIGURE 2   BARREL STORAGE

Another type of pit which can be useful is shown in Fig. 3.

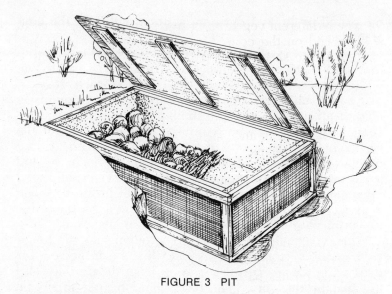

FIGURE 3 PIT

This pit should be located in sloping ground so that excess water drains away promptly. However, one must have a good supply of moisture all the time.

The pit should be neatly dug out; a useful size is six feet long, three feet wide and about two feet deep. (In northern regions maybe this should be deeper; check with your local Extension Service or weather bureau about freezing depths in your area).

Make a box framework of the proper size to fit in the pit and inside the framework stretch hardware cloth tightly. Inside the hardware cloth, line the "box" with styrofoam about two inches thick. The hardware cloth keeps out rodents and the styrofoam insulates.

The top is finished with a two-by-four framework and a tight wooden lid. Obviously, this is all inexpensive if the man of the house does the work.

At harvest time select the vegetables to be stored. Put a layer of clean, washed builder's sand (or clean saw-dust) on the bottom of the pit. Then place (do not dump) a neat layer of root vegetables in the pit and cover that layer with sand or sawdust.

Continue in this manner until the pit is filled. Making a "map" as you work can be very helpful in keeping track of where different vegetables can be found. Bales of straw can be laid on the cover, and this then can be covered with a plastic sheet to keep off the snow. The insulation provided by the straw and styrofoam not only keeps the vegetables from freezing in winter, but also cools them in the warm days of early spring. In early summer the pit should be thoroughly cleaned out, and it should be left open to the fresh air and sun all summer.

Speaking of maps, you will surely want to make one to show where your mounds or pits are located if you live where there is a lot of snow. Better yet, mark them with high stakes. How embarrassed you'd be if you couldn't find some of the produce you so carefully stored!

A "tile" (the construction men's name for a piece of round porous drainage pipe) can be useful. If one 18 inches in diameter and 30 inches high is buried upright in the soil, three bushel baskets of vegetables or fruit can be stored in it. The tile should be located in a well-drained area, away from possible overflow from downspouts and eaves and where it will be shaded. Cover with a deep mulch of straw, hay, or leaves.

The pit, mound, or tile storage methods are clearly not for those who want their produce very handy to the kitchen, or for those who think it would be too great an effort to shovel snow in the northern climate.

Perhaps you'd rather try ordinary barrels, or cartons, which make fine storage containers. As before, handle and pack vegetables with care in sand, sawdust, or leaves. Cover carefully and leave in the garage, or on the back porch. However, watch out for those below-freezing temperatures.

GROUND STORAGE It is very possible to leave some of your root crops in the ground where they grew, until spring. We know of a man as far north as Connecticut who leaves all of his root crops in the ground. He mulches them heavily with 12-18" of leaves, and once a week goes out to dig up a week's supply of vegetables. Because of the thick layer of leaves which keeps the ground warm, he never has to chop through frozen earth to reach them.

If you live in a climate where you believe you could

try this method, you might want to do it in combination with pulling some of your root crops for storage above ground, just to hedge your bets. Then in late winter you may have some fresh, crisp vegetables right out of the ground if you're lucky.

Traditionally, parsnips, horse-radish, and salsify are best left in the ground long enough for thorough freezing, which improves their flavor. Harvested in the late winter or early spring, they provide a great taste treat.

Much less well known is the fact that kale, so rich in vitamin C, withstands extremely cold weather very well and is a perennial. If the plants are well-mulched before snow falls, they will keep throughout the winter and be the first crop to grow in the spring. I have actually seen snow and mulch pushed aside from kale in the late winter and a crop harvested.

This is an important fact for your family's nutrition, as in late winter and early spring your root crops are beginning to lose large amounts of vitamin C.

Ground storage for a long period is also possible for celery and Chinese cabbage. Since these vegetables cannot be canned or frozen successfully, every gardener yearns to keep them as long as possible in the fall. The following methods are those which are recommended for providing you with your own celery or Chinese cabbage well through Thanksgiving and Christmas, if you're both careful and lucky. These vegetables will blanch themselves in the dark.

Method 1

Celery or Chinese cabbage plants of late-maturing varieties may be stored for one or two months in the garden by banking a few inches of soil around the base of the plants at the end of the growing season; build the bank up to the top of the plants before severe freezing occurs. As the weather becomes colder, cover the banking with straw or corn fodder held in place by boards.

Method 2

Another way to store these vegetables is to dig a trench 10-12″ wide, about 24″ deep and any desired length.

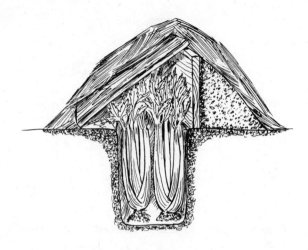

FIGURE 4   CELERY STORAGE

Dig the plants when they are fully grown. Take a clump of soil with the roots and pack the plants in the trench. Water the plants as you put them in the trench and leave the trench open long enough for plant tops to dry off. Unless the soil is very dry at the time of storing, or extended warm weather follows it, you do not have to water again.

Make a sloping roof for the trench by setting a 12″ board on edge beside the trench; bank soil against the board. Then put boards, poles, or cornstalks (from which the tops have been removed) across the trench with one end resting on the upright board and the other on the ground. Spread a light covering of straw, or some similar material that will pack closely, over the roof. As the weather becomes colder, add more covering. Celery stored in this way should keep until after Christmas.

Method 3

You can also store celery or Chinese cabbage in a hotbed.

First, remove surplus soil from the hotbed and substitute a covering of boards for the sash. Then pack the vegetables in the hotbed in the same way that is described for storing in a trench in Method 2.

FIGURE 5   CELERY AND CHINESE CABBAGE STORAGE

Method 4

Celery and Chinese cabbage may also be stored on the floor of a basement storage room, or in any outdoor storage cellar. For this kind of storage, take the plants from the garden just before freezing occurs. Dig up the roots with a clump of soil, set the plants on the floor with the roots down and pack them tightly. If moderately moist, the vegetables will keep well for a month or two.

Do not store celery in a close space with turnips or cabbages: they taint the flavor of celery.

Endive, kept in a storage cellar under conditions described above, will keep for two or three months. When storing, tie the leaves together to help blanching.

CABBAGE STORAGE   Cabbage may be stored in the cone-shaped mounds (as in Fig. 1), or in long pits (as in Fig. 4). The advantage of a long pit is that you can remove a few heads of cabbage without disturbing a whole mound.

To store cabbages in the long pit, pull the plants out by the roots, place them head down in the pit and cover them with soil.

You can also store cabbages upright in a shallow trench that is framed with stakes or poles and covered with straw.

To store cabbage in this way, pull the plants out by the roots and set them side by side with their roots in the trench, packing the soil around the roots. Then build a

FIGURE 6 CABBAGE STORAGE

frame about two feet high around the trench. This frame may be made of boards, poles, or of stakes driven into the ground. Next, bank soil around the frame, and finally, place poles across the top of the frame to hold a covering of straw, hay, or corn fodder.

To store cabbages in a long mound, pull the plants out by the roots, place them head down in the mound and cover with soil as shown in Fig. 7.

FIGURE 7 CABBAGE STORAGE

Heads of cabbage may also be stored on shelves in an outdoor storage cellar, but you probably won't want to keep them in your basement because cabbage odor is likely to permeate your house.

Cauliflower and Brussels sprouts may be pulled and replanted in trenches in the same way as cabbage.

By now it is apparent to you that the foregoing methods of common storage of root crops, celery, cabbage, and some fruits, while not always easy to manage, are very inexpensive. If this is your first year or so of garden-

ing, these methods offer you alternatives to building, or
having built, a real root cellar in your home until you have
the time and inclination to do so.

I may be a repetitive bore, but I'm going to say it again
because it's so important: unless you are certain that your
area is cold enough for these kinds of storage, don't
bother. I want you to use, not lose your stored foods.

If you have just moved to a different part of the country, better check with your local weather bureau and/or
your State Extension Service for information about average winter temperatures and ground-freezing depths in
your area before making any decisions.

INDOOR STORAGE

"Well, there's nothing like the old-fashioned root cellar"
is a frequent comment among people who have lived on
farms all their lives. For those who haven't, but are now
learning how to (or are thinking about it), I wish you the
luck of a young couple I know who left New York City
and bought an old farmhouse in Vermont. Only after they
had bought and lived in it, did they discover (while clear-
ing out debris and remodelling) that what they had naive-
ly believed to be an ordinary storeroom in the basement
(which was full of rubbish), was, in fact, a fine old ma-
sonry root cellar with an arched ceiling. A local mason
looked at it with admiration, saying that it would cost
$5,000 to build today. O.K., maybe you won't have this
luck, but I have several suggestions for you, all of which
will cost far less than $5,000.

Let's begin with some general rules which apply to
all indoor storage.

1. Handle all produce with care while harvesting and
don't plan to store any that is bruised or damaged in any
way. Yes, I know I said this before, but it is terribly important.

2. No matter how simple or sophisticated your indoor
storage space is, some control of temperature, humidity
and ventilation is necessary to insure adequate keeping
of your produce in A-1 condition.

3. Vegetables stored in root cellars like a dirt floor better than a concrete one.

4. Do make plans, however simple, for keeping your containers of produce off a concrete floor (if that's what you have) and away from concrete walls. Direct contact with concrete causes mildew. If you don't have shelves and a slotted wood floor, just blocks or strips of wood to set containers on will do—anything which affords a breathing space between your containers and the concrete.

5. Whatever indoor storage space you use must be kept clean. Get rid of any produce immediately that shows signs of decay. At least once a year, remove all containers from the storage area. If you use cardboard cartons, use new ones each year. If your containers are wooden, clean and air them thoroughly before re-using. Wash the ceiling, walls and floor of the storage space and air it thoroughly during the summer months before re-using.

TEMPERATURE AND VENTILATION   As mentioned in rule 2, the regulation of temperature, ventilation and humidity must be carefully considered. Two thermometers are advisable, preferably of the kind that record minimum and maximum temperatures. Place one outdoors and the other in the coldest location in your indoor storage space. Regulate the indoor temperature by the opening and closing of doors, windows, or other openings used as ventilators.

Outdoor temperatures well below 32°F. are necessary to cool storage air to 32°F. and maintain that temperature. Once cooled to 32°F., the indoor temperature will rise again if ventilators are closed, even though the outside temperature is about 25°F. Close ventilators tightly whenever the outdoor temperature is higher than the storage temperature.

Both indoor and outdoor temperatures must be watched closely, as in most regions daily adjustment of ventilators is necessary.

Temperature requirements for stored crops and the temperatures at which they freeze are given in Table 2.

It's handy to keep in mind that heat rises which means that the temperature of the shelf space will vary. You should store produce requiring warmer temperatures on the higher shelves and so on downward. That produce requiring the coolest temperatures should be nearest the floor.

HUMIDITY A summary of humidity requirements for stored crops is also found in Table 2. Without proper moisture, stored vegetables and fruits shrivel, lose quality and eventually become unfit to eat.

Three ways of maintaining proper humidity are: 1) the use of water: in pans under the ventilators, or by sprinkling the floor frequently, or keeping the floor covered with damp straw or sawdust. 2) The use of damp (not wet) sand, peat, or sphagnum moss for packing the produce in containers, and 3) the use of ventilated polyethylene bags and box liners. One of our Garden Way associates says that dry sawdust requires no additional source of humidity.

You may wish to try a combination of these methods to determine which one you prefer. If you choose not to use damp materials for packing, with the exception of sawdust you will almost certainly have to have another source of moisture in your storage space to avoid the shrivelling of your produce.

CONTAINERS If you use dry sand, sawdust, or leaves for packing your produce, few containers are more useful than your old friend the cardboard carton, obtained from your grocery or liquor store. One Garden Way expert especially likes these containers since no cost is involved and they are never re-used from year to year. In addition, they can be recycled by shredding and adding the material to the compost pile.

Crates, pails, baskets and barrels are all in good standing as storage containers, while bins are in question. Some authorities say "Dump the produce into bins", but I take a very dim view of this advice since it reverses the sound principles that produce be carefully handled to avoid bruising and that no unit of produce stored indoors, except potatoes, should touch another. To wit: each beet, carrot and so on should have some packing material

surrounding it. What do you think? I say, let's *not* dump
the produce into bins.

FACILITIES A well-ventilated basement under a house
with central heating may be used for ripening tomatoes
and for short-term storage (i.e., a few weeks) of potatoes,
sweet potatoes and onions. In general, however, there is
too much heat and too little humidity in modern open
cellars for them to be very satisfactory for any long winter storage purposes.

If your house has an outside stairwell into the basement, this area can be used for some storage with rela-
tive ease and small expense. Install an inside door to the
steps to keep out basement heat; and if you want to cre-
ate an even larger storage area, build inward into the
basement, taking care to insulate the extra well space.
Temperatures in the closed stairwell will go down as
you go up the steps, and a little experimenting with a
thermometer will help you determine the best levels for
the different crops you are storing. If the air is too dry,
set pans of water at the warmest level for extra humidity.

In a pinch, window area wells can be utilized by covering the well. If basement windows open inward, access can be convenient and simple during the cold winter months.

If you are not deterred by the expense involved, a
storage room within your basement can be built at very
reasonable cost, particularly if the man of the house does
the work himself.

There are almost innumerable plans extant for such storage rooms—far too many to include here, so we'll discuss
a simple, effective one built by a Garden Way associate. It
was incorporated into his plan for a new house and so could
be exactly as he believes it should be. He chose a north-
east corner of his basement (the location always recommended), with no heating ducts running through it. If there
had been, he would have insulated them. He planned a
6' x 8' square area, 8' high. He then had two concrete
walls, which he did not cover; and he put up 2' x 4'
studding for the other two walls, which he made of
sheets of waterproof compressed insulation board. He covered the ceiling with this same insulation. A snug-fitting

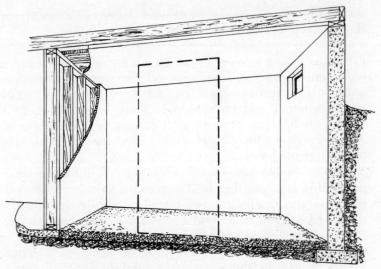

FIGURE 8   BASEMENT STORAGE ROOM

door completed the room, and he figured his costs (at 1971 prices) at about $80, plus his own labor. He will add shelves of rough, cheap lumber.

As I said, there are a great many ways in which a satisfactory storage room can be constructed and your State Extension Service can assist you with any number of plans and some good advice.

If you yearn to keep up with the Joneses, you can always buy a sauna. That's right. I didn't believe it at first, but for vegetable and fruit storage one sauna manufacturer will sell you a sauna 4' x 6' x 6'6" (sans heater and benches) for around $700. They will add shelves for you at no extra charge. This is for indoor installation, but if you want it outdoors, the price is approximately $750 and must be placed on a concrete slab or some form of foundation. Larger saunas cost more, of course.

When you have decided upon what indoor storage facilities you wish to use or build, you will need to know something more definite about storing different vegetables and fruits.

INDOOR STORAGE OF VEGETABLES

MISCELLANEOUS ROOT VEGETABLES Root crops such as beets, carrots, kohlrabi, rutabagas, turnips and so on should not be put into storage until late fall. Late maturing varieties should be planted for this purpose. These crops withstand autumn frosts and are better off in the garden until the nights are cold. Turnips withstand hard frosts and may be left in the garden longer than most other crops. However, they are damaged by alternate freezing and thawing.

Dig the crops when the soil is dry. Beets and carrots should be left on the ground for three or four hours to dry out well. Cut the tops of all crops to within two or three inches of the crown, and make sure all produce is cool before storing. You are then ready to put them away in your basement room. By the way, turnips and rutabagas give off strong odors, and you may prefer to store them outdoors in one of the ways discussed in the section on outdoor storage.

Root crops keep best at temperatures between 32°-40°F. Continued storage at much above 45°F. will cause them to become woody and sprout new tops. All root crops keep their cripness longer when bedded in dry sawdust, or moist sand, peat, or sphagnum moss.

If you find it easier to do so, polyethylene bags may be used.

ONIONS Onions must be mature and thoroughly dry to keep well in storage. Proper field drying is important as was mentioned before. Damaged onions and those with thick necks keep poorly.

Store them in a well-ventilated place and keep them in ventilated containers. A touch of European elegance (and common sense) is provided by braiding the tops of bunches of onions together and suspending them on hooks, from a beam.

Slight freezing will not harm onions, if they are not handled while frozen.

PEPPERS Mature, firm, green bell peppers picked just before frost can be stored for two or three weeks if properly handled. They need high humidity and a temperature of 45°-50°F. They will decay rapidly at lower temperatures. This information comes from several authoritative sources. So, just to confound me, a man told me the other day that his peppers had been stored ten weeks and were still firm and free of decay! The problem is, so far as passing on any advice from him goes, he isn't at all sure why they are keeping so well. They are in a dark place where there is no moving air, and he must have found just the right combination of temperature and humidity.

Hot peppers can be stored easily after they are dry, and they can be dried in two ways:

1. Pull the plants and hang them up.
2. Pick the peppers from the plants and string them up on a line.

Store the dried peppers in a cool, dry place, but not in the cellar.

POTATOES Potatoes that are to be stored require special handling when harvesting. Dig them carefully and remove them promptly from the garden to prevent sun and wind damage, says one of my sources, although more than one experienced farmer leaves his potatoes on the ground three or four hours during a sunny, dry day before storing.

If late blight is present, delay digging until potato vines are dead and dry.

POTATOES, EARLY When early potatoes are harvested, cool storage conditions are difficult to maintain. After harvest, "cure" them by holding them in moist air for a week or two at 60°-75°F. After curing, decay is not likely to be a problem, if you store at 70°-75°F. (but not higher, or they will sprout). A storage temperature of 60°F. would be ideal for keeping early potatoes four to six weeks.

In areas that have mild temperatures in summer, early potatoes can be left in the ground until fall and dug as needed. However, this is not practicable if you live in an area with high temperatures and heavy rainfall, as the crop will rot.

If you do leave these potatoes in the ground, bank or ridge the soil around the plants when you cultivate in late summer. This will allow good drainage and will protect the potatoes from light, which causes them to turn green.

POTATOES, LATE   Late-crop potatoes are better for long-term storage than the early ones. After harvest, cure them in moist air at 60°-75°F. for one or two weeks, then lower the temperature to about 40°F. for winter storage.

These potatoes keep best in moderately moist air, in the dark (to keep them from turning green), and basement or outdoor storage will hold them well for several months. If the temperature becomes too high (55°F. or so), the starch will turn to sugar and the potatoes thus become too sweet.

POTATOES, SWEET   Sweet potatoes, well-matured, carefully handled and cured, can be kept all winter until April or May at temperatures of 55°-50°F. They are easily cut or bruised and should be handled as little as possible. It is best to harvest them directly into storage containers on a cool, dry day.

Cure the potatoes by holding them under moist conditions for two or three weeks at room temperature—about 70°F. Maintain high humidity during the curing process by covering the potatoes with a heavy cloth or paper. After curing, move the potatoes into the storage area where a temperature of about 55°-60°F. can be maintained. Sweet potatoes are damaged by chilling and 50°F. or below is too cool.

Bulk outdoor storage is not recommended because dampness encourages decay in this vegetable.

PUMPKINS AND SQUASHES   These vegetables cannot be kept well in any form of outdoor storage, but with proper care will be good keepers indoors for many months. Most pumpkins keep well; acorn, Hubbard, butternut, buttercup, and even zucchini squashes keep the best. Immature butternut squash will ripen in storage and be as nutritious as those harvested when mature. All pumpkins and

squashes should be cut (leaving an inch or two of stem) before frost.

They will keep better for a long time if they are cured for about ten days at room temperature (i.e. about 70°F.). Curing hardens the rinds and heals surface cuts; however, bruised areas cannot be healed.

After curing, store the pumpkins and squashes in a dry place at 55°-60°F. A shelf up off the floor is the best place, and do not let the vegetables touch one another. Temperature is important, as at 50°F. or below, the vegetables may be damaged by chilling. Above 60°F. they become dry and stringy.

Acorn squashes are an exception to the above suggestions. They must not be cured as they will turn orange, dry and stringy. However, stored in a dry place at 45°-50°F., they will keep well for about six to eight weeks.

TOMATOES By the way, do you recall that earlier I said there are exceptions to the rule that only vegetables picked in their prime should be stored or preserved? One of the exceptions refers to tomatoes which cannot withstand the first killing frost. When frost threatens, green or partially-ripe tomatoes may be harvested and ripened indoors. These will provide you with slowly-ripening goodies for many weeks.

Tomatoes taken from nearly-spent vines usually are not as good as tomatoes from vigorous vines and are more subject to decay. Hence, plant some of your tomatoes rather late in the season so that the vines will still be vigorous when you are ready to harvest. When outdoor temperatures start to range between 32°-50°F. in your area in the fall, harvest the tomatoes within four to five days to prevent damage by chilling.

One of my sources says that when you pick your tomatoes you should remove the stems to prevent them from puncturing other tomatoes, and that you should then wash and dry them (not brush off soil as that causes sand-scarring which leads to decay). Separate green tomatoes from those that show signs of red and pack in single layers in different shallow containers so you'll know which can be used first.

Remember we told you about differing opinions on the subject of common storage? Another source here at Garden Way says tomatoes for storage should always be cut from the vine leaving some stem on to prevent bleeding. The tomatoes should be neither brushed nor washed, he says, but laid carefully on some kind of tray (or any flat surface), in a cool, dry place and covered with newspaper. Peek about every seven to ten days and use tomatoes as they ripen. You will probably have fresh tomatoes well into late November.

Mature green tomatoes reach an eating-ripe stage in about two weeks if held at 65°-70°F. temperatures. Ripening can be slowed down by holding the temperature at 55°F. which means that they will need 25-30 days to ripen; 50°F., for more than a few days, is too chilly. An airy cellar, with moderately moist air and temperatures of 55°-60°F., is best.

Wrapping each tomato individually in foil or polyethylene is another method that is used successfully, since it prevents shrivelling and reduces the moisture loss. However, it may increase decay. If you have a lot of tomatoes to store, checking wrapped ones for ripeness frequently could be a bit of a chore, it would seem.

Here again, you will choose the method that seems most practical for your own situation.

INDOOR STORAGE OF FRUITS

Again I emphasize that vegetables and fruits should never be stored together since fruits readily absorb vegetable odors. Also, fruits require lower temperatures for good keeping than do vegetables. About 31°-32°F. is fine, but do guard against lower temperatures or you will have frozen fruit.

Many major fruits do not store well in the home. Of the ones that do (principally apples and pears), the varieties vary in keeping quality. You will be best served by checking with your local Extension Service about the varieties grown in your area.

As was said so often about the storage of vegetables, careful handling of the fruit to be stored is important. Also, never store a unit of fruit that shows any sign of bruise or decay. Use that up right away.

APPLES   Apples can be stored successfully if the weather turns cold soon after harvest. In many sections, temperatures remain moderate for a month or more after the normal harvest dates of some varieties. Varieties that mature in September, for example Grimes, Golden and Jonathan, cannot be kept long. Golden Delicious, Delicious, McIntosh and Stayman will become overripe in three or four weeks if temperatures are not below 50°F. You see these varieties on the market throughout the winter and spring because commercial growers and packers have especially humidity-and-temperature-controlled storage.

Winesap and Yellow Newton are among the best keepers, often lasting from five to eight months very satisfactorily. Northern Spy, Arkansas Black Twig, Baldwin, Ben Davis, Cortland and Black Beauty are next in line as good keepers and will be satisfactory for four to six months.

Pick apples when they are mature, but still hard. Red apples should be well-colored when harvested. Don't store apples that have glassy spots in the flesh, known, as "water core."

Apples keep best in any area that can be cooled by frosty night air in the fall and can be maintained at about 31°F. for as long as they last.

They can be stored in many ways (barrels or boxes),

but must be protected from freezing, or from too dry an atmosphere which causes shrivelling. Moderate humidity is required.

CITRUS FRUITS If you can keep your storage area down close to 32°F., but not freezing, these fruits will keep well for a few weeks.

PEARS For proper flavor and texture, pears must be picked when fully mature, but still hard and green; then ripened after harvest. Pears are ready for picking when they change color from dark to pale green.

Bartlett, Kieffer, Bosc, Comice and Hardy varieties ripen rather soon after picking and are usually stored by canning. Hardier varieties that will keep for several months in the same conditions of temperature and humidity as apples are Winter Nelis, Anjou and Easter Beurre.

You can judge from what you've read in this chapter that successful common storage requires a lot of common sense because of all the variables. Experimenting can be adventurous, so do try it. You'll probably have more successes than failures.

Three
DRYING

So you want to know about the drying of vegetables and fruits; and why not?

Drying is probably the oldest method of food preservation. Primitive man, from the earliest time when he first harvested edible plants, must have become aware of the fact that certain crops, such as cereal grains, beans and peas, naturally matured and dried while still attached to their stalks. He also must have observed that, in this dried form, some produce could be stored for considerable periods.

In imitation of this natural process, early man developed drying as a practical art to preserve other plant products, as well as meat and fish.

Fruits, such as dates and figs, mature with a naturally high sugar content and with a very low moisture content. These undoubtedly were among the first food products to be dried.

Spices were anciently grown in the East and in the dried form were used very early. Then they finally came to be used in the Western world, to relieve a monotonous diet.

In the early history, drying developed empirically. There was no knowledge of the basic factors involved in preservation, or the factors affecting rate and extent of moisture decrease. Furthermore it's only in the past fifty years that laymen have been hearing and learning so much about the importance of vitamins in their food.

During World War II, when sugar was rationed and canning equipment hard to come by, home economists all over the country studied and published a great deal about drying produce. Then, at the end of the war when items of all kinds were easier to find, and with the advent of the home freezer, drying went out of style.

Well, let's face reality. Freezing and canning are easier methods of food preservation than is drying. I won't fudge on that.

But speaking of facing reality, there are many knowledgeable people today, in 1972, who predict that this country is fast approaching a point of severe power shortages. I don't mean to sound like a prophet of doom. I just want to point out the importance of our knowing how to preserve foods by some other method than the handy-dandy freezer, in the event that we need to, or want to.

At any rate, you may wish to start home drying right now, as a supplement to your other forms of storage. Dried apples, corn and herbs are three kinds of home-dried foods that have always been popular. However, root vegetables and leafy crops, as well as some fruits and berries, can also be preserved by this method. But we do not recommend that you preserve all your surplus produce by drying. Why not experiment at first with drying only a few things, or very small quantities of several kinds of produce? Then, if they are liked, you can expand your drying efforts next year. At any rate, your diet should be varied by the use of fresh vegetables, such as those you have in common storage or purchase.

PRINCIPLES OF DRYING   Drying preserves food by removing the moisture which may support the growth of bacteria or fungi capable of decomposing foods. In addition to moisture removal, drying serves to prevent decomposition by microbial activity.

NUTRITIVE VALUES   You are concerned, as you should be, about the nutrition which dried vegetables and fruits will provide for your family. The proteins, carbohydrates and minerals are probably unchanged if good drying and storage procedures are followed. Much of vitamin A is retained for a while, but is gradually lost. Thiamin is well-retained unless the food is treated with sulfur. And here we have Hobson's choice, for that elusive vitamin C is destroyed in drying unless there is sulfur treatment.

Riboflavin is well-retained if foods are properly stored in the dark, and niacin content apparently is not affected at all in the drying process or in storage.

ADVANTAGES OF DRYING   In this method, as is obvious, a large amount of water is removed from the product, thus reducing its bulk and weight. This makes it possible to store large quantities of food in small spaces.

The costs of drying versus canning compare very favorably. Dried foods are convenient to use, easily prepared for the table, and add variety to the diet.

DISADVANTAGES OF DRYING   It's only fair to tell you that drying foods has some drawbacks. First, the man of the house (unless the woman is much cleverer than I!) must construct some equipment (we provide various plans later in this chapter). To the best of my knowledge there are no home model dehydrators on the market today, although there were in World War II. You may get lucky and find one of these in someone's attic, or at an auction. At any rate, some of the suggested plans are quite simple, while others are somewhat more sophisticated.

Another drawback is that the drying process, while not complicated, is very time-consuming. Also, the flavor of the finished products will be different from the fresh or frozen; they have flavors of their own which are no less pleasing for being different. Do not expect home-dried produce to taste like that which is commercially dried. No homemaker could afford the very pretentious equipment used by commercial driers.

Dried food is going to deteriorate somewhat in storage, even under the best conditions, both in flavor and nutritive values.

Don't be discouraged by all this. You can have an exciting new food adventure. I just thought I should tell it like it is, so that you won't feel it's all your fault that the process doesn't always go smoothly, or the result doesn't taste just as you expected. The disadvantages mentioned have been known by authorities for a long time.

Before starting on an extensive drying program, you should know whether or not your family likes dried foods and what foods are suitable for drying. An acquaintance of mine tried drying spinach once and reported that the taste was so horrendous that she and her family couldn't stand it—and they all like spinach.

You will find among the plans given for driers a very simple, inexpensive one which you might like to try using for your first attempts at drying. And, as previously mentioned, you will probably be best served by trying out the drying method on a small scale at first to see how you like the results.

SELECTION   First, let me emphasize that no method of food storage, including drying, is going to improve the quality of any product. So, good quality in dried products depends on the use of fresh, ripe, firm, perfectly clean foods. One spot of decay in any product may give the entire lot an undesirable flavor. Choose your produce as though for serving at the table. Care should be taken in handling the produce to prevent bruising.

Fruits are easier to dry than most vegetables. The higher sugar content makes them easier to preserve, and they give up water more easily than do vegetables. In general, fruits most suitable for drying are apples, pears, peaches, apricots, cherries, plums, figs and berries.

The best vegetables for drying are sweet corn, mature beans and peas and sweet potatoes. More difficult to dry (but not impossible) are such vegetables as asparagus, greens, celery, cauliflower, green peas, snap beans and okra.

This is not to say that other fruits and vegetables can't be dried, as will be described in detail later.

PREPARATION   Following the selection of your first-quality produce, you should prepare it for drying as rapidly as possible. Two hours from picking to the drier is a good rule. To prevent discoloration of foods as much as possible use stainless steel knives for cutting. Use a clean wooden cutting board, and cut the food into uniform slices or chunks. Have everything ready so that there is no time lag between the cutting and any treatment preliminary to drying.

Regarding this preliminary treatment: every living organism contains enzymes. This is no place for a biology lesson, but it is important for you to know (for the purposes of drying and other storage methods except common storage) something about enzymatic action. Unless it is halted by blanching or pre-cooking in some way before storage, the enzymes will cause the produce to continue to develop. This growth is slowed naturally because of removal from the plant or tree, but it does continue. By extrapolation then, we can see that produce can become woody, overripe, flavorless and finally full of bacteria growth, unless the enzymatic action has been halted before storage.

For drying, onions and herbs need no pre-cooking, but all other vegetables and fruits do. Some fruits may be sulfured, or treated with salt water. Specific directions will tell you which ones.

In case you don't know, or never cared, blanching means plunging the cut produce in boiling water for the required time, then into cold water for one minute, then drying carefully. Or, you can blanch with steam (always my preference over boiling since it preserves certain vitamins and minerals that might leach out in boiling).*

To steam, place the food in a wire basket over one inch of briskly boiling water in a large covered kettle until the product has been steamed the length of time specified in Table 3. If you have a pressure cooker, you may place the basket of food in that for steaming, but leave the petcock open and the cover unclamped.

SULFUR All of you who have purchased commercially dried fruits have noted the lovely natural color, and have probably noticed also, on the label, that they had been treated with sulfur. This is exactly what has preserved their color, and as I mentioned in the section on nutritive values, sulfuring also helps fruits retain vitamin C, although it destroys vitamin B_1.

The fast-growing number of people who prefer to have no preservatives or additives in their foods will want to

* There is no truth to the rumor that I am known to my associates as "Vitamin Vera."

give sulfuring a miss. After all, you can get loads of vitamin C in the tomatoes you canned and the cabbage you stored. And if your fruit is dark, you won't care, so long as you know it's because you skipped the sulfuring.

I should mention, however, that some authorities maintain that sulfuring not only stabilizes color and vitamin C, but also inhibits the growth of molds, bacteria and insect eggs during the drying process and throughout storage.

For those of you who wish to use sulfur, which is recommended for those fruits that darken so easily (such as apples, peaches, pears and apricots) here are two ways to do it:

For small quantities you can immerse them for 30 minutes in a solution made of three ounces of sodium bisulfite or sodium sulfite (both can be purchased at a drugstore) to five gallons of water.

For larger quantities, sulfur dioxide may be used. This too, can be purchased at a drugstore, and you will want about a teaspoon for each pound of fruit.

The fruit is placed loosely on wooden or fabric-bottomed trays. Better not use metal, because the sulfur fumes will corrode it. Trays should be stacked one above another with about three inches of space between each.

Sulfuring of this kind should be done outdoors. The sulfur itself should be on a metal lid or pan at least ten inches below the stack of trays. Also, there should be space between the ground and the pan of sulfur to allow for air combustion. Be sure the sulfur is burning well; then cover the racks tightly with a box, tub, or keg which will enclose the fumes. It is important that the fumes reach all parts of the mass of fruit.

If you have chosen to build the drier shown in Figs. 11 and 12, you can simply move it outdoors and use it for the sulfuring process. All you need add is the metal lid or pan to contain the sulfur.

Sulfuring is completed when the flesh of the fruit takes on a rather uniform semi-translucent appearance and the juice tends to ooze out. The smaller the pieces, and the more mature the fruit, the less time is required for sulfuring. You can probably plan on 10-20 minutes.

INSTEAD OF SULFURING   There are a couple of other ideas I know about to keep fruit from darkening completely. One is to immerse them in a salt-water bath (one tablespoon of salt to each quart of water) for 15 minutes. This helps some.

Also, immediately after pitting apricot and peach halves, they may be steamed on a rack until the skins lift away from the flesh. In this way, peeling and blanching are combined. Steaming promptly after halving aids greatly in overcoming the tendency of the fruit to turn brown.

DRYING METHODS   Now that we've discussed the preparation and treatment of foods for drying, we have to get them dried, don't we? And quickly.

There are various methods for accomplishing this, and your choice will have to be determined by your own inclination, plus your local climate.

Of course, sun-drying is the oldest method, and in the right climate, is by far the simplest. This method consists of putting the product in single layers on trays (or window screens), covering them with cheese cloth or screening to keep out insects, and setting the whole business out in the hot sun. Stir the material several times during the day. It will take all of one day (even in an arid climate) and perhaps two, to dry your product (tests for "doneness" are discussed later). Those of you who live in a hot, arid climate should not hesitate to try it. But don't forget to bring in your trays before sundown to avoid any humidity, and probably put them out the next day.

I am reliably informed that even here in cool Vermont a generation ago, Italian immigrants were drying mushroom slices and tomato paste in this manner. However, wherever you live, it's obvious that if your product is just at its peak for harvest and it's a rainy week, you're not going to get much sun-drying done.

If you would like to try sun-drying in a somewhat more sophisticated way there is a plan in Fig. 8 for a solar drier which is inexpensive to build.

I will also be recommending (with sketches and suggestions for building) a drier to use on top of the stove,

(Figs. 11 and 12), one for the oven (Fig. 10), and an electrically operated one (Fig. 13).

I have a correspondent who lives in Arizona, a very dry climate. He has built his own forced air drier, as shown in Fig. 13, and some for his friends. These driers do not include the heating elements or thermostat. He reports that his and others have been used several years with excellent results, and that they are liked in preference to heat drying. Nevertheless, I point to his home climate, which I believe has a strong effect on his success.

It is perfectly possible to use a drier in your oven inexpensively, provided you are prepared to sacrifice other uses of it for 10-12 hours and be a clock-watcher. Trays for this procedure should be wooden frames covered with coarse cotton cloth. A thin coating of oil on the cloth will prevent materials from sticking. In a gas oven, preheat to 150° and leave the oven door open, but watch to be sure the flame doesn't go out.

The trays of food should be moved to different positions every half hour to assure even drying. This usually means moving the top tray to the bottom, then reversing the middle trays and so on, or whatever regular routine you work out.

In an electric oven, the top unit should be removed, unless that is just the broiler unit. Set the thermostat for 200° for the first hour, then turn it down to 150°. If there is an air vent, the door may be closed; otherwise it should be left slightly open. The trays of food should be moved to different positions every half hour, as recommended for drying in the gas oven.

I am as price-conscious about electric power as the next woman, and I was very skeptical about the cost of drying in my electric oven, so I checked it out with the power company. At 1.3 cents per k.w.h. it costs only about 20-25 cents to keep the oven going at 150° for 12 hours. Nice surprise in this age of inflation. Our local charge is 1.3 per k.w.h. and yours may be less or more, but it gives you a basis for making your own estimate.

In addition to the solar and oven driers I have mentioned, I have had expert assistance (and I needed it!) in choosing which of many available drier plans to recommend to you. I am assured that each one of them can be built by

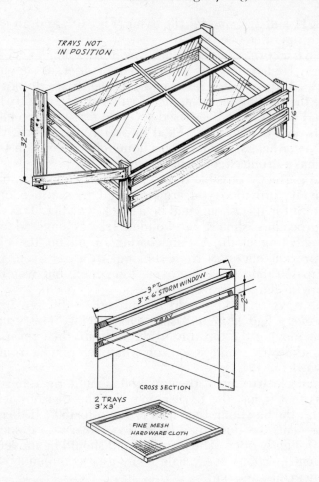

FIGURE 9 SOLAR DRIER This drier is based on a 3 by 6 foot storm window sash. If you use one of a different size, adjust the dimensions to fit.

All lumber is nominally 1 x 4 inches (actually ¾" x 3½") except for the tray frames which are made of ¾" by 1". Make the sides first by cutting the legs to the length shown and nailing the window and tray supports to them, then nailing the braces on the opposite side of the legs.

The long horizontal pieces can be secured to the leg assemblies with screws making them easier to remove for storage of the drier. Notice that the two pieces in front stick up a little beyond the window frame and tray supports to provide a ledge to keep them from sliding forward.

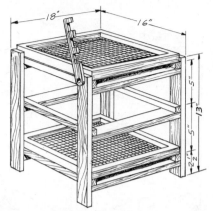

FIGURE 10 OVEN DRIER In the drawing, the center tray has been omitted to clarify the construction. The uprights and cross pieces are made of 1" x 2" wood. The tray slides are ¾" x ¾" and the tray frames are ¾" by 1" wood. All ovens are not the same size and you may have to modify the dimensions to fit yours.

The notched piece is to hold the oven door partially open. Use ½" or ¼" plywood and cut 2" x 2" notches 1" apart. Fasten to the drier with a single screw so that it can be dropped down to engage the oven door. The tray bottoms are made of fine mesh hardware cloth.

Do not set the drier directly on the oven bottom. Put an oven rack in the lowest position. If the legs drop through the wire frames of the rack support them by placing a flat baking sheet or pieces of metal under the legs.

FIGURE 11 TOP OF THE STOVE DRIER This can be used on top of a range or over any burner. The sides are made of 1" × 4" wood lined with homasote, a ½" thick insulating building board, with the ¾" × ¾" tray supports nailed in position on the inside. The top and back are made of ½" plywood nailed to the sides. The door, hinged on one side, can also be made of plywood. Notice the 8" wide sheet metal overlaps the bottom of the drier by 2" and extends the full perimeter of the box. The baffle is a piece of sheet steel 17" x 24" hung with wires attached to the inside with screw eyes.

The trays are made a little narrower than the inside of the box and 4" shorter. When they are put in position the lowest is as far as possible, touching door when it is closed, and the next to lowest tight to the back. Alternate each tray in this manner to allow the air to circulate as shown by the arrows.

This drier can also be used over a portable oil or electric heater by building a stand as suggested in Fig. 12. The dotted line represents the bottom of the drier in position. The height of the top rail should be the same as the top of the heater you plan to use.

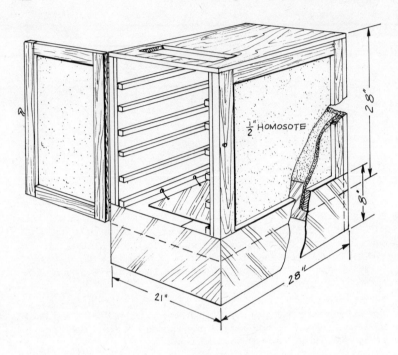

$\frac{1}{2}$" HOMOSOTE

28"

8"

21"

28"

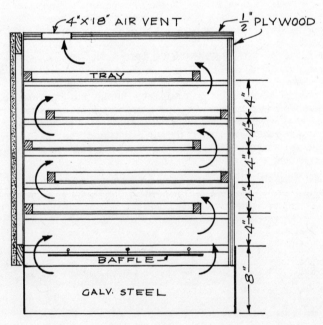

4"x18" AIR VENT

$\frac{1}{2}$" PLYWOOD

TRAY

4" 4"

4" 4"

4" 4"

BAFFLE

8"

GALV. STEEL

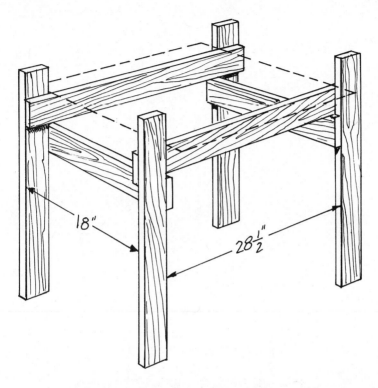

FIGURE 12   STAND TO CONVERT ON STOVE DRIER

FIGURE 13   ELECTRIC DRIER   The electric drier is made much like the top of the stove drier with the exception of an open compartment below in which to slide the fan and motor assembly. This assembly is mounted on a separate piece of ½″ plywood supported by two ¾″ x ¾″ strips of wood so it can be slid in under the drier. The fan has a 6″ diameter blade and a low speed motor and is mounted on a piece of plywood supported at each end by triangular braces. The porcelain sockets for the 5 200 watt bulbs are mounted about 6″ apart with the thermostat as far back as possible. Keep the wiring underneath the board as much as possible.

The door is ½″ plywood hinged on one side with a vent hole cut in it and a slide made of ¼″ plywood mounted over the vent. As in the top of the stove drier, the trays are made four inches shorter than the depth of the dryer. The lowest tray is placed in the drier touching the back, the next tray as far forward as possible and the remaining trays alternated.

In dry hot climates, this drier can be used as a forced air drier by omitting the heating elements and thermostat, using the fan alone.

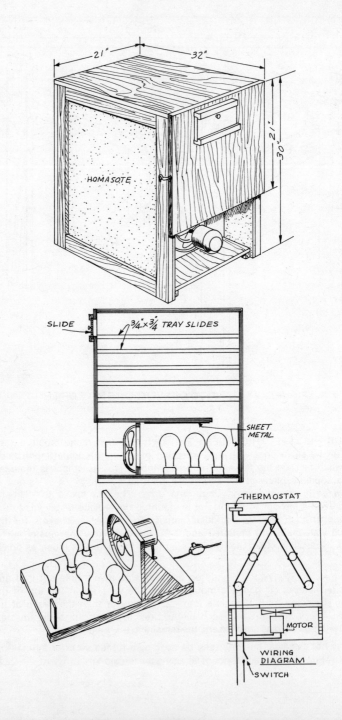

someone who is only fairly handy with tools. I prefer
not to quote any prices, as they vary so much throughout
the country from year to year. I will say that the cost of
materials for each of the driers is in the very low bracket;
in some instances, under $20, say, at current prices.

When you've decided on what kind of drier you want
to start with, and you know about preparing the produce
for drying, you'll need to know more details about drying individual products. Table 3 on page 46 is given for your
easy reference.

WHEN IS THE PRODUCT DONE? No matter what method
you use for drying you should try to avoid temperature
lags or spurts. If you have too little heat you'll have sour
foods; too much and you'll scorch or toughen them.

Watch out for a condition known as "case hardening."
This occurs when the drying temperature is too high with
too little humidity; the outside of the product gets dry
even though the cells within have not yet had a chance to
release their moisture.

One thing you should be aware of in your testing for
proper "doneness" in any of your produce is that not all
pieces will have dried equally. During the drying process
when the product becomes highly wilted and shrunken
it is good economy to turn or stir and expose new sur-
faces to the warm air. When large pieces are being handled,
as in the case of whole plums or cherries, or halves of apricots, peaches, or pears, it is very important to turn them.

Pieces should be removed from the drier as soon as they
are dry. If you find some pieces of the same batch are
dry, and others still moist, remove the dry ones and leave
the others until they're finished.

When one of the larger pieces of fruit is cut through
at the thickest part, the interior should be of the same waxy
or leathery texture and appearance as the rest of the piece.

You will remember that in the chapter on common
storage I mentioned that there is not total agreement
among authorities on methods? Research reveals that this
is true in drying for storage also.

As before, I think it wise to present opinions which differ,
so that you can make your own informed choices. The

TABLE 3

HOW TO PREPARE AND DRY VEGETABLES

Item	Preliminary	Subdivision	Blanch	Time Min.	Special Treatment	Drying Temp.	Finished Characteristics
Beans, snap	Wash, stem	Cut, if desired	Steam	20		150°	Tough to brittle
Beets	Wash, leaving ½" stems	After pre-cooking slice, shred, or cube	Omit		Pre-cook until done	150°	Brittle to hard
Broccoli	Wash and inspect	Half or quarter lengthwise	Steam	15		150°	Tough to brittle
Cabbage	Trim	Slice or shred	Steam	12		140°	Crisp to brittle
Carrots	Wash, scrub with brush	Slice or quarter	Steam	8-12		160°	Brittle or hard
Celery, leaves	Wash	Slice or shred	Steam	15		140°	Crisp
Celery, stalks	Wash	Slice or shred	Steam	15		140°	Tough to brittle
Corn, sweet	Husk	On cob, or cut from cob	Steam	15-20	If dried on cob, should be shelled when brittle	150°	Hard and brittle
Onions	Skin	Slice	Steam	5-7		130°	Crisp
Parsnips	Wash, peel, trim	Slice or cube	Steam	10		150°	Slices brittle, cubes hard
Peas	Shell, wash	Whole	Boiling water	3		140°	Hard, wrinkled
Peppers, green	Halve, core, wash	Half or quarter	Steam	10		150°	Brittle to crisp
Pumpkin, or Squash	Wash, stem, cut open, seed, peel	Cube or slice	Steam	15		150°	Tough
Spinach	Trim off roots, wash well	Whole leaves	Boil	2		160°	Crisp
Turnips or Rutabagas	Wash, peel	Slice or cube	Steam	7		150°	Tough to brittle

HOW TO PREPARE AND DRY FRUITS

Item	Preliminary	Subdivision	Blanch	Time Min.	Special Treatment	Drying Temp.	Finished Characteristics
Apples	Wash, peel, core, trim	Slice	Steam	10	Steam blanch immediately upon slicing, or sulfur	150°	Springy to brittle
Apricots	Wash, halve, pit, peel if desired	Half	Steam	10	Same as apples	140°	Leathery
Cherries, sour	Pit and drain	None	Steam, or none	8-12		130°	Tough
Figs	Stem	Half unless small	Steam	1	Sulfur if desired	120°	Tough
Peaches	Wash, halve, pit, peel if desired	Half	Steam	8	Sulfur if desired, or treat as apples	140°	Leathery
Pears	Wash, peel, core	Half or quarter	Steam	8	Sulfur if desired	140°	Leathery
Plums	Wash	Half unless small	Steam	6		140°	Tough

difference in opinion about drying occurs over a procedure known as "conditioning." Some home economists believe that your dried product should be stored immediately in airtight containers before any moisture can be reabsorbed. Others state that food taken from driers is seldom uniformly dry; and, as any moisture at all will cause mold, it is necessary to obtain an even degree of dryness. They say that this can be done by placing the product in deep containers and stirring once a day for about ten days. Then the products should be re-heated for about half an hour at 150°-180°F. to prevent insect infestation. Following this, store in containers.

STORAGE   Whether or not you have chosen to condition your dried produce, there is no argument on how it should be stored. The containers must be airtight in all cases, but need not be purchased especially. Any tins or glass jars which have tops that can be well sealed will be perfectly adequate.

If you do use glass jars, remember to store them in the dark, as light will affect the product adversely. Using glass permits you to examine the contents from time to time for any signs of insects or of moisture showing on the glass. These are the twin enemies of dried foods. Any sign of either will warrant opening and re-heating the dried product to 165°F. Then re-seal in a fresh container.

All containers of whatever kind should be stored in a cool, dry place.

You will be better served if you use containers small enough so that you can use all the contents at once after opening.

Most properly dried, correctly stored foods will remain in edible condition for about a year, with the exception of dried greens. They are apt to lose their color and nutritive value if stored much over four months.

REHYDRATION: OR NOW YOU PUT BACK THE WATER   All dried foods, except greens, must be soaked in water before cooking. Tests have shown that it is better to put dried vegetables and fruits to soak in boiling water, not cold or lukewarm. This is known to shorten the cooking **time,** with less loss of nutrients; and what's more, it improves the flavor. Use only enough water for your product to absorb readily in soaking and cooking so that no food values are lost; don't over-soak or water-log it.

Most products will absorb 1½ to 2 times their own volume of water. If this quantity of water is absorbed before soaking time is up, add more. Soaking time will vary according to the dryness of the product. Fruits may require anywhere from one to five hours or more. Vegetables will require less time. Small pieces of food need less time for soaking than do large ones.

The best way is to experiment. Soak a medium length of time: if it has not been soaked long enough, it will require a long time to cook until tender. If the cooking time seems excessive to you, increase your soaking period next time you use the product.

Of course, you know you don't pour away the soaking water: you cook with it. Your sink drain simply doesn't need those vitamins and minerals.

When cooking, do cover the pan because the steam helps to "plump up" any pieces that aren't covered with water. Cook over low heat and simmer—don't boil—until the product is tender. Season all vegetables just as you would fresh ones. Fruits are usually cooled, sweetened to taste, and served like the canned varieties.

HERBS No chapter on drying would be complete without a section on the drying of herbs, although it is a far different and simpler procedure than that of drying vegetables and fruits.

Considering the extraordinary costs of those little glass jars of dried herbs at the grocer's, it is well worth the time of any gardener to grow and dry his or her own, and there are several books available on this subject. Even if you start with just a parsley bed, you'll soon want to branch out into growing and drying many other herbs for your winter cooking.

For drying, herbs should be gathered when the plant begins to flower, but the leaves are still green and tender. The young leaves at the tip of the plant are the most flavorful.

For best results, gather the herbs on a sunny morning and dry them rapidly in a well-ventilated room out of direct light. Tender-leaf herbs, such as sweet basil, tarragon and the mints especially need drying out of the sun to hold their color and flavor and to prevent mold.

Thicker, tougher herbs such as rosemary, sage, thyme and parsley have a lower moisture content and may be dried partially in the sun and finished in a lukewarm oven.

Cut the stems of all herbs four or five inches from the tip. If the leaves are dirty, rinse lightly in cold water and drain thoroughly. Tie the stems in small bunches and hang to dry, or spread them thinly on a screen in a dark, airy spot. Drying will take a few days.

When drying is completed the leaves should crumble easily. Strip them from the stems and pack them in airtight containers. Label. If you use glass containers, store them in a dark place or the color will fade from the leaves. A cool cupboard away from the area of your stove is recommended.

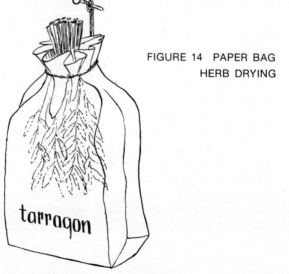

FIGURE 14   PAPER BAG
HERB DRYING

tarragon

Another method for drying herbs—it's a space saver too—is in paper bags. After washing the herbs, tie them in loose bunches of a size you can hold conveniently in one hand. Allow to drip dry, then place in a larger paper bag with the mouth of the bag tied around the stems. Label the bag. The herbs hang free within the bag and none of the oils are absorbed by contact with the paper, as is the case if you store herbs in cardboard boxes. No dust settles on the bunches, and the daily changes in humidity do not affect the herbs. Hang the bags on a wooden clothes dryer, or on coat hangers in a closet.

It may take two weeks for the leaves to shrivel. Open a bag and feel the foliage to see if it is ready to crumble. If so, roll the bag gently between your palms until most of the leaves have dropped off. Pick a time for this when you can work smartly, as if the aromatic herbs lie in the bottom of the bag for any time some of the flavorful oils will be absorbed by the paper. You will have to separate the bunch to pull off leaves from the inside stems, but if a few leaves crumble at your touch the whole bunch is ready.

With either open air or paper bag drying, once the herbs are off the stems, test them to see if they will break up readily by crushing them through a coarse strainer. If they do not, place them on a cookie sheet in a cool oven (100°F.) until they are chip dry. Never try to force herbs to break up if they are slightly flabby. They should fall off the stems easily without a general breaking up of the stems when they are ready for storing. It is hard to remove pieces of broken stems from the dried herb after crushing.

Some people feel that keeping leaves whole or in large flakes until they are to be used preserves the flavor-bearing oils better. In general, however, home grown herbs are so superior in flavor and strength to purchased seasonings, they can be safely ground or crushed before storing. Grinding them in a mortar with a pestle, or rubbing them over a coarse screen are two easy methods of crushing them. Or, you can place a coarse strainer over a bowl and rub the leaves through by hand.

It's fun and handy to have some herb mixtures for specific uses all mixed together before storing. The following suggestions will give you some ideas and you can make up some of your own, as I'm sure you'll want to.

HERB MIXTURES Bouquet garni: bay leaf, thyme and parsley or chervil.

For spaghetti sauce: oregano, basil and crushed hot red pepper.

For tossed salads: sweet basil, chervil, garlic, chives, sweet marjoram, French sorrel.

Ravigote: tarragon, chervil, chives and burnet.

Fish flavoring: basil, parsley, dill, or French tarragon, bay leaf.

Stewing herbs: savory, marjoram, rosemary, lovage.

Poultry stuffing: sage, thyme, marjoram, lovage and parsley.

SUMMARY OF ALL DRYING STEPS

1. Use good quality products in prime condition for eating.

2. Sort and prepare products carefully.

3. Blanch, sulfur, or otherwise treat the products as suggested.

4. Start drying your products promptly following the treatment, especially the vegetables.

5. Keep required temperatures in drying as uniform as possible.

6. Stir products often, and shift position of the trays.

7. Protect the food from insects and dust.

8. Store dried foods in airtight containers in a cool, dry place.

9. Cook foods in water used for rehydration only long enough to make them tender.

Four
CURING AND SALTING

From the meager information available it seems that the Chinese may have been the first to preserve food by the fermentation process. The present day *Yen Tsai*, meaning vegetables preserved in brine, is prepared with mixtures of various vegetables available since ancient times. Turnips, radishes, cabbage and other vegetables were used in these preparations and if available, salt was added. Little was known in regard to the nature of fermentation until relatively recently.

Salt is a very ancient method of preserving all foods, as our ancestors learned that large amounts of it would inhibit spoilage. However, the use of very large amounts of salt means that the product must be freshened by soaking it in several waters. When this is done some of the nutrients are dissolved and lost.

Fermentation occurs with small amounts of salt. Bacteria change the sugars of the vegetables to lactic acid, and the acid with the salt prevents most spoilage organisms from growing. This lactic acid fermentation is the method used in making sauerkraut and other fermented vegetables. Since the salting is so mild, both vegetable and juice may be eaten and thus nearly all nutrient values obtained. About one half of the vitamin C is retained.

Vegetables which may be salted or cured with success are green tomatoes, cabbage, turnips, lettuce (!), peppers, snap-beans, beets, carrots, and cauliflower.

All of these when properly prepared, will be crisp but tender. They are pleasantly acid and salty in flavor; therefore (except sauerkraut), they are good in salads, or served whole on the relish tray without freshening. They are also good when cooked with meat.

GENERAL DIRECTIONS

1. As for all kinds of storage, choose sound, healthy-appearing produce.

2. Follow directions exactly for each product or you won't have good results.

3. Weigh or measure the vegetables carefully, as well as the salt.

4. Do use pure, or "canning" salt. Ordinary table salt usually has iodine and starch added to it. Neither one of these additives is harmful, although sometimes iodine will cause an off-color, and starch will settle to the bottom of the jar giving a cloudy appearance. The best reason of all is that canning salt is much cheaper than table salt.

5. Keep the vegetables covered with brine at all times.

6. Keep the brine surface free from scum and insects.

7. Always throw away any material that is soft or has an off-odor or off-color. This is not fit to eat. (The unpleasant problem of how and why sauerkraut spoils is dealt with after the directions for making it.)

SPECIFIC PRODUCTS

SAUERKRAUT The health-giving properties of sauerkraut have been well-recognized for 200 years or more, and before vitamin C was ever heard of, sauerkraut was a known preventative or cure for scurvy. This was, of course, because cabbage ranks high among foods valuable for vitamin C. Sauerkraut happens also to be very inexpensive to make.

The equipment needed is a scale; a kraut-cutting board, as in Fig. 15. (You can manage with a very sharp knife and ordinary chopping board, but cutting thinly many heads of cabbage will irritate your bursitis and your patience); a large pan; large clean stone jars, crocks, paraffined barrels or quart jars; a round flat paraffined cover; a wooden tamper (or potato masher or a clean heavy bottle); and a clean piece of muslin or cheesecloth.

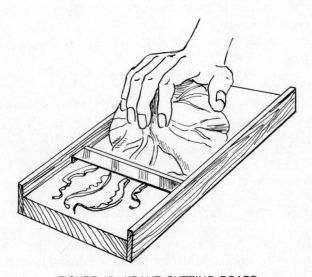

FIGURE 15   KRAUT CUTTING BOARD

All containers should be thoroughly cleaned, sunned, and aired. If you're using a barrel or keg which has held liquids before, it has probably been paraffined to seal the pores of the wood. Do not use wooden containers or covers of yellow or pitch pine, as the kraut will have a piney flavor.

To paraffin your wooden containers, warm them and be sure they are thoroughly dry. Melt paraffin and apply with a brush, thinly but thoroughly. Let dry well.

You will require one pound (two cups) of salt for 40 to 50 pounds of cabbage; approximately 45 pounds of cabbage will fill a 5-gallon crock.

DIRECTIONS FOR MAKING Choose large, firm, well-ripened heads of cabbage and let them stand at room temperature for a day in order to wilt. This causes the leaves to be less brittle and less likely to break in cutting. Trim off outer leaves and wash the heads. With a large knife cut the heads in halves or quarters, and cut up the core to use too (it contains much of the cabbage sugar).

Weigh out about five pounds of cabbage at a time to be cut and measure about ¼ cup salt. This is enough to make at one cutting.

If using a kraut cutting board set the blades to cut shreds about the thickness of a dime. Mix the shredded cabbage and salt thoroughly in a large pan and let stand about five minutes. Not doing so can cause spoilage. Also this step assures that the shreds are less likely to break than if packed at once. Next, pack it into containers by hand and press—don't pound—to draw the juice.

If using large containers, continue with about five pounds of cabbage and ¼ cup of salt at a time until the container is filled within a few inches of the top, tamping each time until juice comes to the surface. You should be careful when tamping not to bruise or tear the shreds of cabbage, as this can result in undesirable softening of the kraut.

Cover the cabbage with several layers of the clean cloth and tuck it down the sides. Then put on your wooden cover (or you may use plastic if you wish). The size of the cover is important; it should just fit snugly within the container. Do not use a plate, as some kraut and juice may be exposed, allowing growth of yeast and aerobic bacteria.

On top of the cover place a weight of such size that the juice comes to the bottom of the cover but not over it. The cloth should be moist, but not covered with juice. The weight needed to keep the juice at a proper height may vary, especially during the first few days of fermentation. Check the kraut often. If juice level is too high, put a lighter weight on the cover, or vice versa. For small containers a bottle partly filled with water serves as a good weight. With this device you can add or subtract weight very easily.

Room temperature of 68°-72°F is recommended for fermenting cabbage, which will usually be ready in five or six weeks. Fermentation will take place faster at 75°-85°F, and at 85°F the kraut will be ready in about two weeks.

A white scum will appear on the brine surface within a few days. This must be removed promptly; if you don't, it will use up the acid resulting from the fermentation and will give bad flavor and odor to the kraut. Lift the cloth carefully so that the scum adheres to it. Wash the cloth and cover, then replace. It will be necessary to remove the scum every day or two. Adjust the weight so as to keep the brine level up. If the brine level becomes too low, make additional brine with proportions of two tablespoons of salt to one quart of water, and add to the kraut.

When fermentation is complete, bubbles will stop coming to the surface. At this time the kraut should be stored in a cold place. It should keep well for three or four months.

You may prefer to use quart jars for storing kraut instead of crocks or barrels. Proceed as given in the directions until the cabbage and salt have stood for the required five minutes. Then fill the jars so that the glass lids force the cabbage down, leaving no air space. Partially seal the jars to allow for expansion of gases during fermentation. This will usually start a day after packing, as you'll be able to see by the formation of gas bubbles on the surface. The best temperature during this process is 70°F, or lower.

During fermentation the gases formed will cause some juice runover. You'd best have set your jars in a pan to catch the juices. In about a week or so, you may have to add more kraut to the jars. For this purpose, you better provide an extra quart of kraut for every four quarts. At the end of ten days seal the jars tightly and allow fermentation to continue. Proper curing will take from four to six weeks. Kraut stored in this way should keep for several weeks in a cold room.

If you expect to keep the kraut for several months you had better can it by the hot pack method.

CANNING, HOT PACK   Since kraut requires little heating, the hot pack method is most efficient and successful. Heat the cured kraut to between 150° and 165°F in its own juice. Add a little water; if necessary as much as one third water may be added to the juice, if there is not enough liquid for canning. Pack in sterilized jars and seal immediately. Set the jars in a pan and cover with water at 150°-155°F, maintaining this temperature for about five minutes. Remove the jars and air cool. If allowed to remain hot for too long a time, the kraut will darken and soften. When canned and cooled properly, kraut will have much the flavor and texture of the raw product. Pass me a Reuben sandwich please!

FLORIDA QUICK METHOD—SMALL AMOUNT   Wash and shred finely the firm cabbage (about one pound will fill a pint jar). To each pound of cabbage add two teaspoons of salt and mix well. Pack in pint jars and place lids on, but do not seal tightly. Place jars in a large pan (not aluminum as it will get stained), and store in a cool place. Fermentation will be completed in eight to ten days. Watch to see when the bubbling stops. When that happens, add enough brine (two tablespoons of salt to one quart water) to cover kraut. Cool and store as in the directions for hot pack canning.

CAUSES OF SPOILAGE   Sometimes, unfortunately, kraut will spoil, i.e. have an undesirable color, odor and/or flavor, or be soft in texture.

Dark kraut may be caused by improperly washed and trimmed cabbage; insufficient juice to cover the cabbage; uneven distribution of salt; exposure to air; or too-high temperatures during fermentation, processing and storage.

Pink color in kraut is caused by the growth of certain types of yeast. These may develop if there is too much salt, an uneven distribution of salt, or if the kraut is not properly covered and weighted during fermentation.

Rotted kraut is usually found at the surface when the cabbage has been insufficiently covered during fermentation so as to exclude air.

So you see (here I go repeating myself!) in this form of storage, as in all others, it pays to follow directions carefully.

LETTUCE KRAUT   Was I ever surprised to learn about this! You too? My sources tell me that head lettuce of the Los Angeles, or iceberg types may be made into kraut in the same manner as cabbage. It is milder in flavor than cabbage kraut and an excellent product if properly made.

TURNIP SAUERKRAUT (SAUERRUBEN) Select young, sweet, juicy purple-topped turnips for this goodie. Peel, shred and after thoroughly mixing ½ cup salt with each ten pounds of turnips, pack in stone crocks. Press turnips down and sprinkle liberally with salt. Fit a tasteless wooden or stone cover inside the crock and weight down as for cabbage kraut.

If turnips are of prime quality, there should be enough juice to cover the top in about 24 hours. Allow to ferment for about 15-20 days at room temperature, keeping the product submerged in brine to prevent discoloration and drying.

Pack fermented turnips in sterilized glass jars and process as for canning sauerkraut.

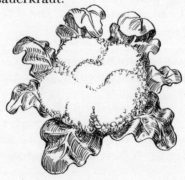

SAUER BEANS, CAULIFLOWER AND GREEN TOMATOES Wash good quality snap beans, snip off ends and cut into short lengths. Scald them about five minutes in boiling water or live steam and cool promptly. Mix, as evenly as possible, a scant ½ cup salt and scant ½ cup vinegar with each five pounds of beans. Pack firmly and proceed with each step as for making sauerkraut.

Cauliflower and green tomatoes (leave small ones whole), may be stored in the same way.

Vegetables prepared by this method will be attractive in appearance, crisp in texture and both slightly salty and acid in flavor. Since they do not need to be soaked in fresh water, they retain a fair amount of nutrients. These vegetables are good in salads or on a relish tray.

Beans and cauliflower should be boiled ten minutes before serving. Discard, without tasting, any material that is soft, or has an objectionable odor.

WEAK BRINING Several vegetables may be stored by this method very successfully. When preparing to serve them they do not need to be soaked to remove the salt; but if the flavor is too tart, they can be rinsed well, or soaked a short time before cooking.

Vegetables that you may use are snap beans, beets, beet tops, carrots, cauliflower, mustard and turnip greens, kale, rutabagas and turnips.

In general, prepare vegetables as for table use by trimming and cleaning. Cut the cauliflower, or break it into flowerets, and slice or dice turnips and rutabagas. Wash greens thoroughly to remove all traces of grit. Wash small carrots and beets, but do not cut them. Wash very tender beans and blanch five minutes in boiling water; or steam, and cool promptly. They may be cut or left whole.

Prepare what is called a five per cent brine. The amount needed will be about half the volume of vegetables to be packed. To each gallon of water add and dissolve ½ pound of salt. This is about one cup. Add one cup of vinegar that has a four to five per cent strength of acetic acid.

Pack the vegetables in clean containers until they are nearly full. Cover with several layers of clean cheesecloth

and tuck in around the edge. On top of this place a
weighted cover. When brine is ready, pour over vegetables until it comes up over the cover.

Store containers in a cool place. Follow directions given
for sauerkraut about removing scum, and washing the
cloths and the cover frequently. After a fermentation period of about ten days, repack in glass jars and proceed as
in canning sauerkraut. If necessary, make more brine to
cover vegetables in the jars.

OTHER METHODS There are methods of heavily salting or
brining the vegetables I have been discussing which you
may care to explore for yourself. They are not included
here, as in order to prepare them for the table, it is necessary to soak them one or more times in fresh water for
12-14 hours. Since this does a pretty good job of pouring
nutrition down the drain, I do not care to recommend
either of these methods. There is an abundance of other,
better methods of storing your vegetables from which you
and your family will derive the utmost in nutrition. I re-
fer to those discussed in this and other chapters.

Five
CANNING

Will you be proud of the attractive jars filled with vegetables and fruits that you canned? Or will you be unhappy because the food is not covered with liquid and has become dark? Or do some of the jars have sediment in the bottom?

Properly canned foods are attractive in appearance and very nutritious. Even people who have freezers usually do some canning too. This is because some vegetables (primarily tomatoes) and fruits, such as pears and peaches, lend themselves especially well to canning in preference to freezing.

Canning has the advantage of being less expensive than freezing. Apart from the wide difference in the original cost of equipment, there is no constant operating cost after the food is canned.

You will need to replace some jars and lids from year to year when they become defective, but this is not a major cost item. Rubber rings should be new each year.

Canning is not difficult. It's just like anything else you learn to do; seeming hard and time-consuming at first, then much easier after you get the hang of it.

IT'S IMPORTANT TO DO IT RIGHT! Unless you understand what takes place in the cannning process, you won't see why you must use certain equipment and be so careful about processing temperatures and times.

Foods spoil whether in jars, in your refrigerator, or on the kitchen shelf, because they are under constant attack by spoilage organisms. These are bacteria, molds, and so on, which are always present in air, water and soil.

Also, vegetables and fruits contain enzymes which help to bring about normal ripening. However, unless the

enzymatic action is halted, it continues on to cause over-
ripening; changes in flavor, color and texture; and eventually, spoilage.

When you can vegetables and fruits, you must heat
them through at proper temperatures and time to destroy
the spoilage organisms and stop the enzymatic action.

Clear?

The main thing to remember is that each step in the
canning process is important; one step depends on another for successful results.

PLANNING   Planning ahead for one's canning and having
all equipment checked and ready is as important as the
canning itself. Besides, it makes you feel so virtuous.

Weeks ahead of the canning season, it's good organiza-
tion to make a list of the kinds and amounts of foods
you're going to need and want. The following Table 4 is
given for you to use as a rough guide if you're new to
canning. Making out a list gives you a concrete way to plan
a variety of your family's favorites.

You should not can more than your family can easily use
within a year.

TABLE 4
FOOD PLANNING GUIDE

Product	Number Times Served	Approximate Size Serving	Amount Needed One Person	Amount Needed Family of 4
Citrus fruit and tomatoes (Includes juices)	7 per week— 36 weeks	1 cup	63 quarts	252 quarts
Dark green and yellow vegetables Broccoli, spinach and other greens, carrots, pumpkin, sweet potatoes, yellow winter squash	4 per week— 36 weeks	½ cup	18 quarts	72 quarts
Other fruits and vegetables Apples, apricots, peaches, pears, asparagus, green beans, Lima beans, corn, green peas, summer squash, etc.	17 per week— 36 weeks	½ cup	76 quarts	304 quarts

EQUIPMENT For those of you who have never canned
before, I'll spell this out as carefully as I can. The equipment falls into two categories: that which is essential,
and that which is not essential, but nice to have.

In the essential category is a steam-pressure canner,
which, aside from your jars and lids, is the one most important thing you'll need.

FIGURE 16 CANNING PRESSURE COOKER Cut-away view shows jars
in postion.

You will also need a jar lifter, a funnel, a ladle with a
lip, a food mill, large measuring cups, large trays and a
wire basket. You will need to decide on what types of containers you are going to use. There are several on the market to choose from, and you should buy the sizes that
best fit your family needs. These will generally be pints and
quarts. Buy them early in the season when the stores are
well-stocked; then you'll risk no disappointment later. If
you have the time or inclination, go to some farm auc-
tions. You're apt to find cartons of canning jars going at
very low prices.

The following Table 5 will help you to determine the
number of containers you may need.

TABLE 5

JAR ESTIMATING

Raw Produce	Measure and Weight	Approximate Number Quart Jars Needed	Approximate Amount Needed For 1 Quart Jar
Fruits			
Apples	1 bu. (48 lbs.)	16-20	2½ to 3 lbs.
Applesauce	1 bu. (48 lbs.)	15-18	2½ to 3½ lbs.
Apricots	1 lug or 1 box (22 lbs.)	7-11	2 to 2½ lbs.
Berries	24 quart crate	12-18	1½ to 3 lbs.
Cherries	1 bu. (56 lbs.)	22-32 (unpitted)	2 to 2½ lbs.
	1 lug (22 lbs.)	9-11 (unpitted)	2 to 2½ lbs.
Peaches	1 bu. (48 lbs.)	18-24	2 to 3 lbs.
	1 lug (22 lbs.)	8-12	2 to 3 lbs.
Pears	1 bu. (50 lbs.)	20-25	2 to 3 lbs.
	1 box (35 lbs.)	14-17	2 to 3 lbs.
Plums	1 bu. (56 lbs.)	24-30	1½ to 2½ lbs.
	1 lug (24 lbs.)	12	1½ to 2½ lbs.
Tomatoes	1 bu. (53 lbs.)	15-20	2½ to 3½ lbs.
	1 lug (30 lbs.)	10	2½ to 3½ lbs.
Tomatoes (for juice)	1 bu. (53 lbs.)	12-16	3 to 3½ lbs.
Vegetables			
Beans, Lima (in pods)	1 bu. (32 lbs.)	6-10	3 to 5 lbs.
Beans, Green or Wax	1 bu. (30 lbs.)	12-20	1½ to 2½ lbs.
Beets (without tops)	1 bu. (52 lbs.)	15-24	2 to 3½ lbs.
Carrots (without tops)	1 bu. (50 lbs.)	16-25	2 to 3 lbs.
Corn, Sweet (in husks)	1 bu. (35 lbs.)	6-10 (whole-kernel)	3 to 6 lbs.
Okra	1 bu. (26 lbs.)	16-18	1½ lbs.
Peas, Green (in pods)	1 bu. (30 lbs.)	5-10	3 to 6 lbs.
Spinach and other greens	1 bu. (18 lbs.)	3-8	2 to 6 lbs.
Squash, Summer	1 bu. (40 lbs.)	10-20	2 to 4 lbs.
Sweet Potatoes	1 bu. (50 lbs.)	16-25	2 to 3 lbs.

From Ball Blue Book, Courtesy of the Ball Corp., Muncie, Ind.

Do use standard canning jars for vegetables and fruits. Jars which have held peanut butter, mayonnaise and so on, may not withstand the high temperatures needed for correct processing.

The four most common types of lids are shown here in Fig. 17, along with directions for using.

It is convenient, but not necessary, to have a food chopper, a blender and a water-bath canner. If deep

METAL
SCREW
BAND

FIGURE 17   JARLIDS

METAL
LID

SEALS
HERE

Put the flat metal lid on the top rim of the jar, with the sealing side down. Put the flat lid on first, then the metal band. Hold the lid down and screw the band on firmly.

METAL
SCREW
BAND

GLASS
LID

RUBBER

SEALS
HERE

This is a self-sealing type. Don't tighten further when you take the jar from the canner, as you may break the seal. Put the wet rubber ring on the glass lid. Place the lid on the jar with the rubber against the top rim. Put on the screw band and screw it down tight. Then turn the band back a little to loosen it slightly. After canning, as soon as you take jar from canner, screw the band down tight to complete seal.

PORCELAIN
LINED
SCREW
CAP

RUBBER

SEALS
HERE

Put the wet rubber ring on the shoulder of the jar. Screw the cap down tight, then turn it back a little to loosen it slightly. As soon as you take the jar from canner, screw the cap down tight to complete the seal.

GLASS
LID

RUBBER

SEALS
HERE

WIRE
BAIL

Put the wet rubber ring on the ledge near the top of the jar. Place the glass lid on the rubber ring. Then, put the lower wire bail over the top of the glass lid so it fits in the groove. Next, push the other wire bail down against the side of the jar. This jar is sealed. Do not disturb the wire bail after canning.

enough, your steam-pressure canner can double as a water-bath canner if you leave the petcock open.

Fig. 18 shows you what a water-bath canner is like. As
you see, there is a metal basket in there to keep the jars
from touching the bottom of the kettle, thus permitting
free circulation of water under the jars. You do not
need to use a basket if you prefer a rack. The canner needs
to be deep enough for water to cover the tops of the jars
one or two inches without boiling over.

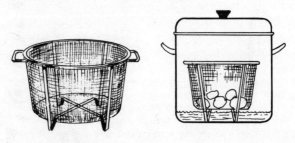

FIGURE 18   WIRE BASKET   for steaming. Use in a pot with a tightly
fitting lid.

I want to remind you that the pressure gage on your
steam-pressure canner should be checked for accuracy
once a year. Your home demonstration agent can tell you
where to have it tested.

Clean the petcock and safety valve openings by drawing a string through them. Do this after each use of the
canner. Then wash the canner and dry thoroughly.

Another preparation you can make ahead (then there'll
be no panic on your canning days) is to examine with
care all your jars and lids. Any of these which are chipped,
cracked or dented should be discarded (for canning purposes) and replaced. Defects prevent airtight seals. Run
your finger around the mouth of each jar to see if it has a
nick.

Also, for your vegetable canning you will probably
want to purchase pure salt, known as "canning" or "curing" salt. For one thing it's cheaper than table salt, and
also it doesn't have any iodine or starch in it. Iodine sometimes causes an off-color in canned vegetables, although
this is not harmful. Starch is sometimes added to table salt

to keep it from lumping. In canning, the starch may settle to the bottom of the jar giving the contents a cloudy appearance, which again is not harmful, but it isn't attractive either.

METHODS: HOW TO AND WHY   There are only three processing methods for canning which are unhesitatingly recommended by authorities. They are the steam-pressure, water-bath and open-kettle methods. The latter two are desirable for certain products only, as I'll explain.

The steam-pressure method is a way of processing foods under pressure at a temperature of 240°F. (ten pounds pressure at sea level to 2,000 above). This method is recommended for all low-acid foods. (See directions for specific foods). The steam-pressure canner is the only kitchen utensil which supplies sufficient heat to destroy bacteria which cause spoilage in low-acid foods.

The water-bath method is a way of processing foods at a temperature of 212°F. This method is perfectly satisfactory for processing fruits, tomatoes and other acid foods. Enough heat is supplied by the boiling water to destroy the bacteria which can cause spoilage in acid foods.

The open-kettle method is safe only for jams, preserves

and pickles, since they contain enough sugar or vinegar to preserve them. In this method, the food is cooked in an uncovered kettle and poured, boiling hot, into hot sterilized jars, then sealed quickly. For vegetables, the temperatures in the open-kettle method are not high enough to destroy all spoilage organisms.

There are two ways in which to fill jars for processing: the cold or raw pack, and the hot pack. In the cold pack the jars are filled with raw food which is then covered with boiling water; then the jars are processed in water-bath, or steam-pressure. The hot pack means that the food is hot and partially cooked when put into the jars before being processed.

In the section of this chapter giving canning instructions for individual vegetables and fruits, it will specify which type of pack should be used; or, in many cases, will offer a choice. Most home canners prefer the hot pack method in general. More food can be packed in a standard canning jar and the time the food stays in the pressure canner is generally less. Often some vegetables "float" if they are not pre-heated before being packed. This does no harm to the food, but it does look unattractive.

UNSAFE METHODS   I don't care if your next-door neighbor does tell you that she's been oven-canning safely for years. This is a dangerous procedure, and I warn you against it. One explosion can damage both person and property. Also, the temperature of the food in jars during oven processing does not get high enough to insure the destruction of spoilage organisms.

I warn you, too, against "cold sealing," which means ignoring any processing of the jars after filling them. It is an unreliable method, as heat is necessary to seal jars properly. Someone is bound to tell you the old wives' tale that you can cold seal foods if you add aspirin. I am certain that the drug industry will agree with me if I emphasize that while aspirin will do a lot for your aches and pains, it does absolutely nothing to kill bacteria in your canned foods.

You will probably hear about some "fabulous" canning powders, or chemical preservative. Don't use them; some are harmful, and none are needed if you process your foods carefully and correctly. Just don't take any shortcuts.

Are you beginning to get the idea that I'm bearing down on safe procedures? You're right, I am. There is nothing dangerous about home-canned vegetables and fruits if you process them correctly. But if you do not, you may wind up with spoilage, which is wasteful.

You should be familiar with the signs of food spoilage

and look for it in each jar you open, since it should never be eaten by humans or animals. Watch for spurting liquid and gas bubbles; soft, slimy or moldy food; cloudy liquid; sediment in the liquid; leaking jars; bulging caps and any unnatural odor or color. Grit your teeth and *throw it away!*

Then there is a possibility that your vegetables can contain a toxin which will cause botulism poisoning. It has no odor and does not change the appearance of the food. This toxin is created by the growth of spores of Clostridium botulinum in a sealed jar. These spores fly around in dust and wind and exist in soil which clings to raw foods. However, the spores cannot grow in the presence of air, nor do they thrive in acid foods. But they do grow and form a toxin in sealed jars of improperly processed low-acid foods. The spores are destroyed when the low-acid foods are correctly processed in a steam-pressure canner.

As an extra precaution, before tasting any home-canned low-acid foods, they should be boiled for 15 minutes. This will destroy any toxin that could be present through an error in processing.

You may be curious as to why the boiling temperature of 212°F. will eliminate the possibility of botulism poisoning, whereas a steam-pressure temperature of 240°F. is recommended (in processing) to kill the C. botulinum spores. This is because the toxin created by any possible remaining spores can be dissipated by boiling.

Many questions will come to your mind about home-canned food, both before and after you've done your canning. The following Table 6 attempts to cover all possible conditions which may arise.

As we all learned in our physics course (or had you forgotten?), water boils at a much lower temperature at high altitudes. This means we must make certain of added time for processing in water-bath, or of added pressure for the steam-pressure method at high altitudes.

The processing times given in this chapter are for foods canned at altitudes less than 1,000 feet above sea level, when using the water-bath. For steam-pressure, the pressure given is for altitudes less than 2,000 feet above sea level. If you live in an area of higher altitudes, check with Table 7 for adjustments in time or pressure.

TABLE 6

WHAT'S THE CAUSE?

Condition (Product Usable Unless Spoilage is Indicated)	Cause	Prevention
Foods darken in top of jar.	1. Liquid did not cover food product. 2. Food not processed long enough to destroy enzymes. 3. Manner of packing and processing did not produce a high vacuum. 4. Air was sealed in the jars either because head space was too large or air bubbles were not removed.	1. Cover food product with liquid before capping jar. 2. Process each food by recommended method and for recommended length of time. 3. Pack and process as recommended. 4. Use amount of head space as recommended. Remove air bubbles by running rubber bottle scraper between food and jar.
Fruits darken after they have been removed from jar.	Fruits have not been processed long enough to destroy enzymes.	Process each fruit by recommended length of time. Time is counted when water reaches a full boil in the canner.
Corn is brown.	1. Corn was too mature for canning. 2. Liquid did not cover corn. 3. Jars were processed at too high a temperature. 4. Variety of corn used.	1. Use freshly picked corn which has plump, shiny kernels filled with milk. 2. Cover corn with liquid before capping jar. 3. Keep pressure in canner at recommended pounds; guage may be faulty and it should be checked. 4. Use different variety next time.
Pink, red, blue or purple color in canned apples, pears, peaches and quinces.	A natural chemical change which occurs in cooking the fruit.	None.
Green vegetables lose their bright green color.	Heat breaks down chlorophyll, the green coloring matter in plants.	None.
Green vegetables turn brown.	1. Vegetables were overcooked. 2. Vegetables were too mature for canning.	1. Time precooking and processing exactly. 2. Asparagus tips should be tight and the entire green portion tender. Pods of green beans should be crisp and meaty and the beans tiny. Peas, Lima beans, and all other beans and peas which are shelled should be green.

Table 6 (Cont.)

Condition (Product Usable Unless Spoilage is Indicated)	Cause	Prevention
Some foods become black, brown or gray.	Natural chemical substances (tannins; sulfur compounds and acids) in food react with minerals in water or with metal utensils used in preparing food.	Use soft water. Avoid using copper, iron or chipped enameled ware, also utensils from which tinplate has worn.
Yellow crystals on canned green vegetables.	Glucoside; natural and harmless substance, in vegetables.	None.
White crystals on canned spinach.	Calcium and oxalic acid in spinach combine to form harmless calcium oxalate.	None.
White sediment in bottom of jars of vegetables. May denote spoilage.	1. Starch from the food. 2. Minerals in water used. 3. Bacterial spoilage . . . liquid is usually murky, food soft. (Do not use.)	1. None. 2. Use soft water. 3. Process each food by recommended method and for recommended length of time.
Fruit floats in jar.	Fruit is lighter than the sirup.	Use firm, ripe fruit. Heat fruit before packing it. Use a light to medium sirup. Pack fruit as closely as possible without crushing it.
Cloudy liquids. May denote spoilage.	1. Spoilage. (Do not use.) 2. Minerals in water. 3. Starch in vegetable. 4. Fillers in table salt.	1. Process each food by recommended method and for recommended length of time. 2. Use soft water. 3. None. 4. None, except by using a pure refined salt.
Loss of liquid during processing. (Food may darken, but will not spoil. Do not open jars to replace liquid.)	1. Food not heated before packing. 2. Food packed too tightly. 3. Air bubbles not removed before capping the jar. 4. Pressure canner not operated correctly. 5. Jars not covered with water-bath canner. 6. Starchy foods absorbed liquid.	1. Heat food before packing. 2. Pack food more loosely. 3. Remove air bubbles by running rubber bottle scraper between food and jar. 4. Pressure should not be allowed to fluctuate during processing time. Allow pressure to drop to zero naturally; wait 2 minutes before opening lid. 5. Jars should be covered 1 inch with water in canner throughout the processing period. 6. None.

Table 6 (Cont.)

Condition (Product Usable Unless Spoilage is Indicated)	Cause	Prevention
Jar seals, then comes open. Spoilage evident. (Do not use.)	1. Food spoilage from under-processing. 2. Disintegration of particles of food left on the sealing surface. 3. Hairlike crack in the jar.	1. Process each food by recommended method and for recommended length of time. 2. Wipe sealing surface and threads of jar with clean, damp cloth before capping. 3. Check jars; discard ones unsuitable for canning.
Jar of food fails to seal. (Correct cause and reprocess the full time or use the food immediately.)	Many factors could be involved, such as failure to follow instructions for using jar and cap, or a bit of food may have been forced up between the jar and lid during processing.	Carefully follow methods and instructions for using jars and caps and for foods to be canned.
Zinc caps bulge. May denote spoilage.	1. Cap screwed too tight before processing. (Condition is evident as jar is removed from canner.) 2. Food spoils from under-processing. (Condition evident after jar has cooled and has been stored from a day to a few months.) Do not use.	1. Screw cap tight, then loosen about ¼ inch before putting jar in canner. 2. Process each food by recommended method and for recommended length of time.
Black spots on underside of metal lid. (If jar has been sealed and then comes open, spoilage is evident. Do not use.)	Natural compounds in some foods cause a brown or black deposit on the underside of the lid. This deposit is harmless and does not mean the food is unsafe to eat.	None.

From Ball Blue Book, Courtesy of the Ball Corp., Muncie, Ind.

CANNING DAY: OR WHAT IS A NICE GIRL LIKE YOU DOING IN THAT HOT KITCHEN? Come now, it isn't going to be that bad. For one thing, why not get up extra early if it's going to be hot? Secondly, don't try to can all day long. It's much easier to process a few jars each day than to work at it too long at a time. Better for your disposition, too. Also, if you've taken my advice, all your canning equipment is

TABLE 7

ALTITUDE CHART

Water-Bath Canner Altitude	Increase Processing Time If the Time Called For Is:		Steam-Pressure Canner	
	20 Minutes or Less	More than 20 Minutes	Altitude	Process at Pressure of:
1,000 feet	1 minute	2 minutes	2,000- 3,000 feet	11½ pounds
2,000 feet	2 minutes	4 minutes	3,000- 4,000 feet	12 pounds
3,000 feet	3 minutes	6 minutes	4,000- 5,000 feet	12½ pounds
4,000 feet	4 minutes	8 minutes	5,000- 6,000 feet	13 pounds
5,000 feet	5 minutes	10 minutes	6,000- 7,000 feet	13½ pounds
6,000 feet	6 minutes	12 minutes	7,000- 8,000 feet	14 pounds
7,000 feet	7 minutes	14 minutes	8,000- 9,000 feet	14½ pounds
8,000 feet	8 minutes	16 minutes	9,000-10,000 feet	15 pounds
9,000 feet	9 minutes	18 minutes		
10,000 feet	10 minutes	20 minutes		

From Ball Blue Book, Courtesy of the Ball Corp., Muncie, Ind.

clean, checked out and organized, so that you're ready to go.

Get out what you need and let's go through the steps of water-bath canning first, which you remember is suitable only for fruits and vegetables high in acid content, such as tomatoes.

1. Prepare salt-vinegar water, or sugar syrup if needed. (See instructions for specific foods).

2. Fill water-bath canner (or steam-pressure canner if that's going to be your substitute) half full of hot water and put it on to heat.

3. Wash your jars and lids in hot soapy water (they need not be sterilized), rinse well, and let them stand in very hot water until you're ready to use them.

4. Select ripe, firm produce (save the "seconds" for immediate table use), and wash and drain. Remove cores, pits, seeds, or skins.

5. Prepare only enough produce for one canner load at a time. Preparation methods are discussed for individual products. Fill jars and cover the food with boiling water, or boiling hot syrup, leaving ½-inch head space. Remove the air bubbles by running a rubber spatula between the jar and the food. If needed, add more liquid to cover. Wipe the top and threads of the jar before capping,

and place each jar as it is filled on the rack in the canner. The water should be hot, not boiling yet.

6. When the jars are in the canner, add water to cover them one or two inches. Bring water to a boil, then reduce heat to hold the water at a steady, gentle boil.

7. Start counting the processing time, and don't guess about this. Be a clock-watcher, or set an alarm for yourself.

Process for the length of time recommended for individual products. If, during that time, the water should boil away and the tops of the jars are above the water line, add boiling water to cover them an inch or two.

I think it's smart to keep a separate kettle of water on the boil for just such emergencies so that the processing time doesn't get fouled up.

When processing time is up, remove jars from the canner (I told you you'd need that jar lifter!), and stand them on wood a few inches apart, out of drafts to cool. Leave for about 12 hours.

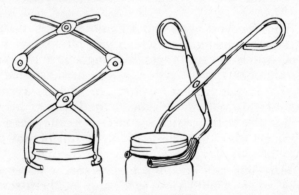

If you're using a steam-pressure canner for the water bath, follow instructions above, except that when the water comes to a boil, you should put the cover on leaving the petcock open for ten minutes. Then close it and bring the pressure up to five pounds for the remainder of the time.

For all your low-acid vegetables you do recall, don't you, that you must use the steam-pressure processing?

Prepare jars and lids as for the water-bath method and the vegetables as directed. Put the jars into the canner

that has two or three inches of water in it (or amount recommended by the manufacturer). Put canner over heat,
lock on the cover, and leave vent open until steam escapes steadily for ten minutes. Close petcock and bring
pressure up to ten pounds. Keep it steady at this point for
the time required for individual vegetables.

When processing time is up, remove canner from heat
immediately. Let it stand until the pressure drops to zero.
Wait a minute or two, then open the petcock and tilt the
cover far side up so steam escapes away from you. Take
jars out of the canner.

Treat them as from the water-bath, by standing them
on wood a few inches apart, out of drafts, to cool for at
least 12 hours.

NEXT DAY JOBS Test the seal on glass jars with porcelain-
lined lids by turning each jar partly over in your hands.
To test a jar that has a flat metal lid, press center of the
lid. If the lid is down and won't move, the seal is tight.
Or, tap the center of the lid with a spoon. A clear, ringing
sound means a good seal, and a dull note usually means
the seal is poor. Store the jars without leaks. If you find
a leaky jar, or one that is only partly sealed, use that food
right away.

If you have the kind of lids with screw bands, this is the
time to remove them, with care. Wash and store them.

Before storing canned food, wipe the containers clean.
It's a little nicety to label each jar with the name of contents and the date canned.

After a week, examine each jar for any leakage, as this
indicates the food is spoiling.

WHERE TO PUT IT NOW YOU'VE CANNED IT Proper storage
of canned foods is important. They should be put in a cool,
dry, dark place. Heat and light affect the color of the foods
and to some extent, the flavor. Dampness may corrode
the metal lids of jars, and eventually cause leakage. If you
have a cool, dry place that is not dark, store the jars in
cartons and cover with paper.

Freezing may crack a jar or break a seal, thus letting in
bacteria.

Properly processed, carefully stored canned foods will retain good quality for a year.

WATER-BATH CANNING OF ACID VEGETABLES AND FRUITS

TOMATOES Use firm, ripe tomatoes which are free of decayed spots, weather cracks and fungus growths. Wash them clean; then scald a few at a time to loosen the skins, and dip in cold water. Cut out core and green spots, then peel.

After the above preparation, tomatoes may be packed cold or hot.

For cold pack, put tomatoes into hot jars, pressing them until the spaces are filled with juice, leaving ½-inch head space. If desired, add ½ teaspoon salt to each quart. Adjust lids. Process pints 35 minutes, quarts 45 minutes, in boiling water-bath.

For hot pack, boil tomatoes five minutes, stirring constantly. Pour hot into hot jars, leaving ½-inch head space. Adjust lids. Process pints 10 minutes, quarts 15 minutes in boiling water bath.

SALAD TOMATOES Many homemakers like to can whole tomatoes for uses in salad. This can be done as follows: prepare tomato juice (see below), or use commercially canned juice. Pack peeled, cored, whole tomatoes into hot jars, leaving ½-inch head space. Pour hot tomato juice over tomatoes, leaving ½-inch head space. Adjust lids. Process pints 35 minutes, quarts 45 minutes in boiling water-bath.

TOMATO JUICE Wash and drain firm, ripe tomatoes. Be sure to cut out any decayed spots, as even a small one will spoil a whole batch of juice. Remove core and blossom ends. Leave tomatoes whole and bake in the oven, or cut in small pieces and simmer until soft, stirring often. Press through a sieve, or food mill. Reheat juice until almost, but not quite, boiling. Pour hot into hot jars, leaving ¼-inch head space. Salt and spices to taste may be added. Adjust lids. Process pints 10 minutes, quarts 15 minutes in boiling water-bath.

SYRUPS FOR CANNING FRUITS

Type	Sugar to One Quart Water	Yield
Light	2 cups	5 cups
Medium	3 cups	5½ cups
Heavy	4¾ cups	6½ cups

If you wish to make a medium syrup with corn syrup, use 1½ cups sugar and one cup corn syrup to three cups water.

To make syrup with honey, use one cup sugar and one cup honey to four cups of water.

To make all syrups, measure sugar and liquid (either water or fruit juice) into a saucepan. Cook until sugar dissolves. Keep syrup hot until needed, but don't let it boil down. Usually 1 to 1½ cups of syrup will be needed for each quart of fruit.

TO KEEP IT PRETTY While preparing fruits such as pears, peaches, or apples for canning you can arrange matters so that the fruit doesn't darken by using ascorbic-citric acid according to the manufacturer's directions. Or, if using pure ascorbic acid, sprinkle ¼ teaspoon to each quart of fruit just before capping jar. Either the ascorbic-citric acid or pure ascorbic acid can be purchased at your druggist's.

Another method for keeping the fruit light is to add two tablespoons each of salt and vinegar to one gallon of water. After you have cored or pitted and peeled the fruit, drop it into this solution. Don't leave it more than 20 minutes, and do rinse the fruit thoroughly before packing.

APPLES Use a light or medium syrup. Wash, drain, core, pare and slice cooking apples. (They may be left in quarters, or halves if you prefer). Treat them to prevent darkening. Drain. Boil in syrup five minutes. Pack hot into hot jars leaving ½-inch head space. Cover with boiling syrup leaving ½-inch head space. Adjust lids. Process pints and quarts 20 minutes in boiling water-bath.

APPLESAUCE Make sauce as you usually do and season to taste with spices and sugar. Reheat to boiling and pour into hot jars. Adjust lids. Process pints and quarts 20 minutes in boiling water-bath.

BERRIES Use the cold pack for berries such as raspberries that do not hold their shape well. Make a light or medium syrup. Wash berries in ice water to firm them. Drain. Pour ½ cup boiling syrup into hot jars. Fill jars with berries. Shake the jars to pack berries loosely without crushing, leaving ½-inch head space. Adjust lids. Process pints 15 minutes, quarts 20 minutes, in boiling water-bath.

Use hot pack for blackberries or others that hold their shape well. Wash, drain and measure ripe berries. Put into kettle: add ¼ to ½ cup sugar for each quart of berries. Let stand for two hours, then cook until sugar dissolves and berries are boiling hot. Pour immediately into hot jars, leaving ½-inch head space. If there is not enough syrup to cover berries, add boiling water leaving ½-inch head space. Adjust lids. Process pints 10 minutes and quarts 15 minutes in boiling water-bath.

STRAWBERRIES These berries may be canned, but you should be warned that they tend to fade and lose their flavor. If you want to try some, use firm, ripe ones which do not have white or hollow centers. Hull, wash and drain the berries. Use ½ to ¾ cup sugar to each quart of berries. Let stand five or six hours in a cool place. Heat slowly until sugar dissolves and berries are hot. Pack immediately in hot jars leaving ½-inch head space. Adjust lids. Process pints 10 minutes, quarts 15 minutes, in boiling water-bath.

CHERRIES If cherries are sweet, make a light or medium syrup; if they're sour, you'll need a medium or heavy syrup. Cherries for pies may be canned in water, but hold their color better when some sugar is used.

Wash, drain and stem the cherries. You may pit them or not, as you choose. If you want to, you can make your own little cherry-pitter out of a paper clip. If you do leave in the pits, prick each cherry with a sterilized needle to prevent bursting and shrinking.

Pour about ½ cup boiling syrup into a hot jar. Fill with cherries. Shake the jar to pack them closely without crushing, leaving ½-inch head space. Cover with boiling syrup or water, leaving ½-inch head space. Adjust lids. Process pints 20 minutes, quarts 25 minutes, in boiling water-bath.

For hot pack, prepare cherries as for cold pack. Measure. Mix ½ to ¾ cup sugar with each quart of cherries. Heat slowly until sugar dissolves and cherries are heated through. If cherries are unpitted, add a little water to prevent sticking. Pack hot into hot jars, leaving ½-inch head space. If there is not enough syrup to cover cherries, add boiling water or light syrup, leaving ½-inch head space. Adjust lids. Process pints 10 minutes, quarts 15 minutes, in boiling water-bath.

GRAPEFRUIT   I can remember when I was a child growing up in cold New England, thinking that in the warmer states the wonderful citrus fruits grew all year long; and wasn't I envious? Now I know that even those of you who are lucky enough to live where you can pick from your own trees can't do that for many months. So why not can some?

Make a light syrup. Peel ripe, heavy fruit, cutting deeply enough to remove white membrane. Run a thin knife between pulp and skin of each section and lift out the pulp, without breaking it if possible. Discard seeds. Cover with boiling syrup, leaving ½-inch head space. Adjust lids. Process pints and quarts ten minutes in boiling water-bath.

PEACHES   Sort, wash and drain just enough ripe peaches for one canner load. Prepare medium syrup. Put peaches in a wire basket and dip them into boiling water for about a minute to loosen the skins. Then dip in cold water and drain. Cut the peaches in half, pit and peel. Drop them into salt-vinegar water, unless you are using the ascorbic-citric acid.

For cold pack, put them in hot jars, cavity side down, with layers overlapping. Cover with boiling hot syrup, leaving ½-inch head space. Adjust lids. Process pints 25 minutes, quarts 30 minutes, in boiling water-bath.

For hot pack, cook a few peaches at a time in syrup until heated through. Pack immediately in hot jars leaving ½-inch head space. Adjust lids. Process pints 20 minutes, quarts 25 minutes, in boiling water-bath.

PEARS Pears should be picked when full-grown and stored in a cool place (60°-65°F.) until ripe, but not soft. Bartlett pears are considered best for canning. The hot pack method should be used. Make a light syrup. Cut pears into halves or quarters, core and pare. Treat to prevent darkening. Drain. Cook pears five or six minutes in hot syrup. Pack immediately in hot jars, leaving ½-inch head space. Adjust lids. Process pints 20 minutes, quarts 25 minutes, in boiling water-bath.

CINNAMON PEARS Add two sticks of cinnamon and a few drops of red food coloring to each quart of syrup. Remove cinnamon before packing pears. Proceed as for plain pears.

MINT PEARS Add oil of peppermint and green food color (a drop at a time) until syrup is flavored and colored as desired. Cook pears in syrup ten minutes before packing. Proceed as for plain pears.

RHUBARB Some say it's a vegetable—some say it's a fruit, but anyway, it's high in acid. So, like tomatoes and the foregoing fruits, it can be processed in a boiling water-bath. Measure. Add ½ to 1 cup sugar to each quart of rhubarb. Mix well and let stand for three or four hours. Heat slowly to boiling and let boil ½ minute. Pack immediately into hot jars leaving ½-inch head space. Adjust lids. Process pints and quarts ten minutes in boiling water-bath.

STEAM-PRESSURE CANNING OF
LOW-ACID VEGETABLES

All of the following are the low-acid vegetables which must have the steam-pressure processing to insure destruction of the spoilage organisms. If you live in an area that is higher than 2,000 feet above sea level, remember to consult the altitude chart on page 73 for the adjustments you should make in pounds of pressure to be used.

ASPARAGUS   This delicious vegetable may be either hot or cold packed. Wash and drain tender asparagus that has tight tips. Remove the tough, woody ends and scales. Wash again. Leave stalks whole, or cut into one-inch lengths. Boil three minutes for hot pack, then put immediately into hot jars leaving one-inch head space. Add a teaspoon salt to each quart. Cover with boiling water, leaving one-inch head space. Adjust lids. Process pints 25 minutes and quarts 30 minutes at ten pounds pressure.

For cold pack, prepare as for hot pack, but do not boil the asparagus. Pack raw into hot jars, leaving one-inch head space. Add one teaspoon salt to each quart. Cover with boiling water, leaving one-inch head space. Adjust lids. Process pints 25 minutes and quarts 30 minutes at ten pounds pressure.

BEANS, DRIED   Use kidney, or any other variety of dried beans. Cover them with cold water and soak for 12-18 hours in a cool place. Boil 30 minutes. Pack immediately in hot jars, leaving one-inch head space. Add a teaspoon of salt to each quart. Cover with boiling water, leaving one-inch head space. Adjust lids. Process pints one hour and 15 minutes, quarts one hour and 30 minutes, at ten pounds pressure.

BEANS, LIMA AND BUTTER Choose young, tender beans and shell them. Wash; then for hot pack, boil them three minutes. Pack immediately into hot jars, leaving one-inch head space. Add a teaspoon salt to each quart. Cover with boiling water, leaving one-inch head space. Adjust lids. Process pints 40 minutes, quarts 50 minutes, at ten pounds pressure. If beans are large, process ten minutes longer.

For cold pack, put the beans loosely into hot jars, leaving one-inch head space. Do not press or shake down. Add a teaspoon salt to each quart. Cover with boiling water, leaving one-inch head space. Adjust lids. Process pints 40 minutes, quarts 50 minutes, at ten pounds pressure.

BEANS, SNAP, WAX AND GREEN Choose young, tender pods. Wash, drain, trim ends and string, if necessary. Break or cut into two-inch pieces, or leave whole if small. Boil three minutes for hot pack. Put immediately into hot jars, leaving one-inch head space. Add a teaspoon salt to each quart. Cover with boiling water leaving one-inch head space. Adjust lids. Process pints 20 minutes and quarts 25 minutes at ten pounds pressure.

For cold pack, put beans into hot jars leaving one-inch head space. Add a teaspoon salt to each quart. Cover with boiling water, leaving one-inch head space. Adjust lids. Process pints 20 minutes, quarts 25 minutes, at ten pounds pressure.

BEANS, SOY Use green soy beans. Follow directions for Lima beans. Process pints 55 minutes and quarts an hour and five minutes at ten pounds pressure.

BEETS Sort dark red beets for size—small, medium and large. Wash. Trim, leaving two inches of stems and the tap roots so the vegetable won't bleed in cooking. Boil each size at a time, until the skins can be slipped off easily. Remove those, and finish trimming; then, according to size, slice, dice, or leave them whole. Pack into hot jars, leaving one-inch head space. Add a teaspoon salt to each quart. Cover with boiling water, leaving one-inch head space. Adjust lids. Process pints 30 minutes and quarts 35 minutes at ten pounds pressure.

BROCCOLI This vegetable, and some others as noted, will usually turn color when canned and will also develop a strong flavor. If you want to can it anyway, wash it well. This vegetable tends to harbor insects, so it's best to soak it in a salt solution for half an hour, using one teaspoon salt to each quart of water. Cut into two-inch pieces; or if desired, leave the stalks whole, in as uniform thickness as possible. Boil three minutes. Pack hot (flowerets up, if broccoli is in stalks) into hot jars, leaving one-inch head space. Add a teaspoon salt to each quart. Cover with boiling water, leaving one-inch head space. Adjust lids. Process pints 30 minutes, quarts 35 minutes at ten pounds pressure.

BRUSSELS SPROUTS See note under broccoli about color, flavor, and insects. Choose ripe green sprouts of fairly uniform size, not larger than two inches in diameter. Wash and prepare as for cooking. Drain. Boil for three minutes in fresh water; then pack while hot into hot jars, leaving one-inch head space. Adjust lids. Process pints 30 minutes and quarts 35 minutes at ten pounds pressure.

CARROTS Wash and scrape carrots and wash again. Slice or dice the large carrots, but why not leave small ones whole? For hot pack, boil three minutes and pack immediately into hot jars, leaving one-inch head space. Adjust lids. Process pints 25 minutes, quarts 30 minutes, at ten pounds pressure.

For cold pack, put the raw carrots into hot jars, packing tightly and leaving one-inch head space. Add a teaspoon salt to each quart and cover with boiling water, leaving one-inch head space. Process pints 25 minutes, quarts 30 minutes, at ten pounds pressure.

CAULIFLOWER See note under broccoli about color, flavor and insects. Clean and separate the head of cauliflower into flowerets of fairly uniform size. Boil three minutes, then pack into hot jars, leaving one-inch head space. Cover with boiling water leaving one-inch head space. Adjust lids. Process pints 30 minutes, quarts 35 minutes, at ten pounds pressure.

CELERY   The raw garden celery you have hoarded in common storage won't stay crisp and tasty for more than a few months, up to Christmas at best. Cooked celery is a tasty vegetable (especially with a gourmet touch like cheese sauce), and we all want it in our soups and stews.

So, if you have an abundance of celery in the fall, better can some for later use.

Wash it well and cut into two-inch lengths. Boil three minutes and pack into hot jars. Add a teaspoon salt to each quart. Cover with boiling water, leaving one-inch head space. Adjust lids. Process pints 30 minutes, quarts 35 minutes, at ten pounds pressure.

CELERY AND TOMATOES   This combination is delicious for use as a table vegetable, or in soups, stews, sauces and casseroles.

Use equal parts of celery and peeled, cored, chopped tomatoes. Add as much chopped green pepper and onion as you like. Without adding water, mix and boil five minutes. Pack into hot jars, leaving one-inch head space. Add a teaspoon salt to each quart, and any other seasoning you'd like, such as some dried basil, oregano and minced garlic. Cover with boiling water, leaving one-inch head space. Adjust lids. Process pints 30 minutes, quarts 35 minutes, at ten pounds pressure.

CORN   This vegetable, like peas, must be gathered and canned at just the right stage of ripeness. The kernels should be plump and shiny; give them the thumbnail test. They should spurt milk. Don't gather it until you are all ready to can, for speed is important from garden to processing. It is best if you work with small quantities at a time.

CORN, WHOLE KERNEL   Husk corn, remove silk and wash the ears. Holding each ear upright and using a very sharp knife, cut the kernels from the cob, but do not scrape the cobs. Measure the corn, and to each quart add one teaspoon salt and two cups boiling water. Boil three minutes, then pack quickly into hot jars, leaving one-inch head space. Adjust lids. Process pints 55 minutes, quarts one hour 25 minutes, at ten pounds pressure.

For cold pack, cut corn off as for hot pack. Pack it loosely into hot jars leaving one-inch head space. Adjust lids. Process pints 55 minutes, quarts one hour and 25 minutes, at ten pounds pressure.

CORN, CREAM STYLE This method of preserving corn is useful for the ears you have which are less than top quality.

Husk corn, remove silk and wash ears. Holding each ear upright and using a very sharp knife, cut down about half way through the kernels. Put this corn into a bowl. Then, holding the ear over the bowl, use the back of your knife to scrape the cobs, thus adding the milk and kernel hearts to the first corn you cut.

For hot pack (using only pint jars), measure the corn and to each pint add ½ teaspoon of salt and 2½ cups boiling water. Boil three minutes, then pack quickly into hot jars, leaving one-inch head space. Adjust lids. Process pints one hour and 25 minutes at ten pounds pressure.

For cold pack (using only pint jars), prepare corn the same as for hot pack, up to the point where corn has been measured. Pack it loosely into hot jars, leaving one-inch head space. Do not shake or press down. Add ½ teaspoon salt to each jar. Cover with boiling water, leaving one-inch head space. Adjust lids. Process pints one hour and 25 minutes at ten pounds pressure.

MIXED VEGETABLES Carrots, green beans, celery and Lima beans (or any other mixture you like) may be canned all together. Prepare each vegetable according to the individual directions, then mix them together. Boil three minutes and drain. Pack while hot into hot jars, leaving one-inch head space. Adjust lids. Process

pints and quarts for the time needed for the vegetable requiring the longest processing. Check individual directions.

MUSHROOMS   If you're one of those knowledgeable and
intrepid souls who knows exactly which mushrooms
are edible, you'll want to pick enough for canning, as
well as for your immediate table use. The rest of us had
better stick to buying them in the stores in the fall
when they are plentiful and relatively inexpensive. How
luxurious you'll feel later, to have your own supply of
canned mushrooms to use in cooking!

To prepare, wash them and trim off any discolored or tough places. Cover with cold water and let
soak for ten minutes to remove every bit of dirt. Break
off stems, and slice all the tender ones, discarding those
which are tough. Leave small mushrooms whole; cut
larger ones in halves or quarters. Steam them for
about four minutes.

Use only half-pint or pint jars. When the mushrooms are steamed, pack into hot jars, leaving one-inch
head space. Add ½ teaspoon salt and ⅛ teaspoon ascorbic acid (to preserve the color) to each jar. Add boiling
water to cover mushrooms, leaving one-inch head space.
Adjust lids. Process half-pints and pints 30 minutes at
ten pounds pressure.

PEAS, FRESH BLACKEYE   Shell and wash these when
freshly gathered. For hot pack, boil them three minutes, then pour into hot jars, leaving one-inch head
space. Add one teaspoon salt to each quart. Add boiling water, if needed to cover, leaving one-inch head

space. Adjust lids. Process pints 35 minutes, quarts 40 minutes, at ten pounds pressure.

For cold pack, after shelling and washing peas, pack them loosely into hot jars, leaving one-inch head space. Do not shake or press down. Add one teaspoon salt to each quart. Cover with boiling water, leaving one-inch head space. Adjust lids. Process pints 35 minutes, quarts 40 minutes, at ten pounds pressure.

PEAS, GREEN Shell and wash these when freshly gathered. Drain, then sort into two groups; large and small. Wash again and drain. The small ones should be boiled only three minutes for hot pack, while the larger ones need five minutes. You might can them separately too, saving the small ones for special occasions like your mother-in-law's visit.

Anyway, when they're boiled, pour them hot into hot jars, leaving one-inch head space. Adjust lids. Process pints 35 minutes, quarts 40 minutes, at ten pounds pressure.

For cold pack, pack the peas loosely into hot jars, leaving one-inch head space. Do not shake, or press down. Add a teaspoon of salt to each quart. Cover with boiling water, leaving one-inch head space. Adjust lids. Process pints and quarts for 40 minutes, at ten pounds pressure.

POTATOES, SWEET This vegetable can be successfully canned by the dry pack method. Use freshly dug potatoes of uniform size and color. Boil, or preferably steam, until the skins can be slipped off. Do not pierce with a fork, but use kitchen tongs or a spoon to lift them. Remove skins. Pack them while hot into hot jars, leaving one-inch head space. Pack tightly, pressing to fill the spaces, as you do not add liquid. Adjust lids. Process pints an hour and five minutes, quarts an hour and 35 minutes, at ten pounds pressure.

SUCCOTASH Boil fresh corn five minutes. Cut kernels from the cobs with a very sharp knife, but do not scrape the cobs. Mix with any proportion of Lima or shell beans that you choose. These should have been boiled three minutes. Pack the mixture while hot into hot jars, leaving one-inch head space. Add a teaspoon salt to each quart and cover with boiling water, leaving one-inch head space. Adjust lids. Process pints one hour and quarts one hour and 25 minutes, at ten pounds pressure.

SUMMER SQUASH, ALL TYPES   Use young and tender vegetables. Wash them well, but do not pare. Cut into thin slices or small pieces. Cook by boiling, or preferably steaming, for two or three minutes. Pack into hot jars, leaving one-inch head space. Add one teaspoon salt to each quart. Cover with boiling water, leaving one-inch head space. Adjust lids. Process pints 30 minutes, quarts 40 minutes, at ten pounds pressure.

ARE YOU PROUD?

If you have followed all the procedures accurately, you will have attractive, nutritious foods for your family. Here's a test you can apply, regarding the general appearance of each jar you've processed.

Is there a good proportion of liquid to solid?
Does the liquid cover the solid, with about one-inch head space?
Are the jars free of foreign matter: stems, cores, seeds and so on?
Are the pieces uniform in size and shape?
Are the shapes retained: i.e., not broken or mushy?
Is the color uniform and good?
Is the liquid or syrup clear and free of sediment?

I do hope you can answer "Yes" to all the questions, and that you are indeed proud of your shelves of canned foods!

Six
FREEZERS AND FREEZING TIPS

I recognize that there is a large group of people, trying to live off the land, which prefers to avoid products of modern technology. They willingly forego cars, even electricity, and so do not wish to employ the elegant sophistication of the food freezer.

However, many of you have freezers, or wish to have. Because you have a garden, you may consider a freezer an indispensable household appliance when your budget permits its purchase.

The chief advantage of frozen vegetables and fruits is that, if properly processed, they will when prepared for the table most nearly resemble fresh produce in taste, quality and appearance.

When you decide to buy a freezer, many questions will arise in your mind. Here are a few answers which I hope will be useful.

FREEZER PURCHASING Many sources give approximately the same general information on this subject. First, you should be aware that the cost of freezing goes beyond the initial purchase price of the freezer. This latter is usually based on cubic foot capacity, style, type (whether chest or upright), and the special features it has.

Do not be misled by over-optimistic advertising which often says that you can store 35 pounds of food in one cubic foot of space. While this is true geometrically, the food you store will not all be in geometrically-shaped packages so that you can fill every corner and crevice. Let's be realistic and pare a few pounds from advertising copy that says "ten cubic feet of freezer space will hold 350 pounds."

If you plan to put nothing but square packages in your freezer, you are probably safe if you plan 32

pounds to the cubic foot. Packaging materials take up
space, and you must plan on space being left for the
necessary expansion in many vegetable and fruit packages.

So, how large a freezer will you need to store your
food? While many manufacturers claim three cubic feet
per person is adequate, I'm afraid they're fudging on
this. Government bulletins and most home economists
recommend that you figure on six cubic feet of freezer
space per family member and I go along with them on this.

It is probably unnecessary to add that while chapter
seven will deal only with the freezing of your vegetables
and fruits you will also want to plan on space for
cooked foods, meat, fish and poultry, unless you're vege-
tarians. The more space you have, the more food in
greater variety will be on hand.

BRANDS   The make you should buy? Uh-uh, I'm not going out on that limb! In my home, when we need to
buy a new major appliance, we consult the justly famous
Consumers' Reports and are guided by what their tests
reveal of different brands. No appliance will ever meet
your needs completely, but you can come to some in-
telligent compromise when you see some objective sta-
tistics.

DECISIONS, DECISIONS!   As you know, there are two general types of freezers: trunk-opening or chests, and
door-opening uprights. Each type has its advantages
and disadvantages, and you will see many models of
each type.

The chest type obviously requires more floor space
than does the upright and before you buy one check
all the measurements with care against measurements
in your house. When it is delivered it may have to go
through several doors, and even down your basement
stairs. It's not much fun to jimmy off door moldings
while men are waiting to move your freezer.

You should consider too the height and arm reach
of the person(s) who will most often be storing or re-

trieving foods. It may be hard and back-breaking to reach out-of-the-way packages in the bottom corners.

Some manufacturers provide interior lights which go on when the freezer lid is raised. This is an important feature to look for if your freezer is to be placed in a dark basement corner.

Most chest freezers contain storage baskets. This feature aids in compartmentalizing one's food storage.

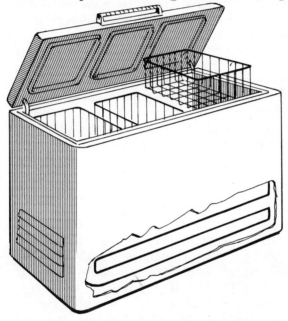

FIGURE 19 CHEST FREEZER The cut-away view shows the freezing coils in the walls. These coils are on all four sides of the freezer. Wire racks roll on tracks for easier access to lower level. Freezers range in size from 10 cubic feet to 22 cubic feet.

In some chest freezers the coiling containing the re-frigerant which permits you to freeze food is sealed into the side walls of the cabinet and occasionally into the floor. This type of chest is called a "wrap-around." Since all foods must be frozen as rapidly as possible, before moving them to the storage areas, it is obvi-ous that the packages must be placed carefully against the sides of the chest, or on the floor of a wrap-around.

In some chest models the manufacturers have provided separate sharp freezing compartments. This feature simplifies freezing in a chest.

Few freezers of the upright type take up much more, if any, floor space than that needed by your refrigerator. If you want one, you will want to consider that in standard manufacture an upright freezer door is right-handed, swinging back to the right when you open it. Do you have space to open the door wide in the location you're thinking of? Left-opening doors are available, but usually only on special order.

When considering upright freezers, it is well to distinguish between those which are simply wrap-around chests up-ended and with shelves added and those which have freezer-plate shelves. The latter are, in my opinion, the primary reason for wanting an upright. There should be three or four such shelves, and they offer the great convenience of being able to place food to be frozen on the shelves as easily as you put food on a cupboard shelf. Each freezer-plate shelf has its own system of coiling.

If you buy an upright which is only a wrap-around, you will still have to freeze your packages of food by placing them in contact with the side walls.

Many freezers come equipped with a visible or audible alarm signal. This alarm can warn you that the current to the freezer is off. An audible alarm for a freezer in the basement is invaluable; a visible one is fine for one in the kitchen, or other area frequently occupied. If your freezer does not have an alarm, one can be purchased and installed.

FREEZER MAINTENANCE COSTS   While you're thinking about the initial cost of a freezer, you should also be alert to the overhead, or maintenance costs. These remain pretty much fixed (except for wrapping materials), regardless of how much or little you freeze.

These include:
1. Net depreciation: the life expectancy of a reputable make will be 12-15 years.

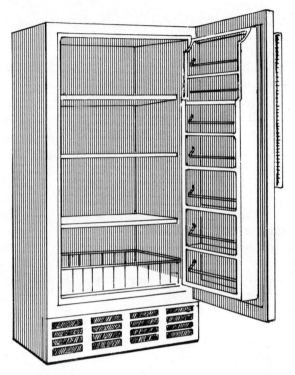

FIGURE 20   UPRIGHT FREEZER   Each shelf contains freezing coils on which food to be frozen is placed. The back of the door is used for frozen juices and other smaller packages.

2. Finance charges, if you pay on the installment plan.
3. Repairs: about two per cent of the purchase price.
4. Cost of electricity to freeze your products initially: this will be approximately 0.1 k.w.h. per pound at 2½ cents per k.w.h. You can look at your electric bill, or check with your power company to determine your local costs per k.w.h. and adjust the foregoing figures accordingly.
5. Cost of maintaining a freezer operating temperature of 0°F, or lower; this can be determined by multiplying 0.22 k.w.h. by the cubic feet of storage space you have, or plan to have. Multi-

ply that total by 2½ cents, or whatever you're pay-
ing per k.w.h. This will tell you what the maintenance cost will be, per day.
6. Packaging costs, which vary, must be considered
as part of your freezer maintenance.

One study on overall costs shows that in a 16 cubic
foot freezer that cost $250 (just to pick some figures),
it will cost approximately 14 cents a pound to store
480 pounds of frozen food, or $67.20, per year. How-
ever, 720 pounds will come to about ten cents a pound,
or $72, and 1200 pounds can be stored for only seven
cents a pound, or $84.

Depreciation and repair costs will be the same whether you store 50 or 1200 pounds.

Your freezer expenses can be reduced by selecting one
which is the right size for your family. A freezer kept
full of food will stay at the proper temperature and
operate more economically than a freezer half full.

Continuous use and replacement of food are the keys
to satisfactory freezer ownership. Like your budget,
your freezer requires good management. Keep a constant turnover; treat it as a checking, not a savings,
account.

For a large family, you might fill a freezer three or
more times a year. The average family should have a
complete turnover of most items twice a year.

Your goal on management of this appliance is to
make it return a good share of its purchase price and
operating expense.

EQUIPMENT FOR FREEZING O. K., so you've bought a
freezer. Now you need to know what equipment to
have on hand before starting to freeze anything.
Probably you have a good deal of it already. You will
want several very sharp knives of various sizes; a cutting board; a large pot (at least 8-quart capacity) with
a strainer insert and a tight cover, for water blanching;
a rack, or trivet for steam blanching; enough packaging
material to contain all you prepare; and plenty of ice
for cooling the vegetables after blanching.

BASIC RULES Do use high quality foods. There is no magic in freezing, and it will not improve the quality of any food. If you freeze tough old string beans because you can't bear to throw them away, you'll eat tough old string beans.

Follow directions closely when processing for freezing. Speed is important. A good motto to follow is "Two hours from picking to freezer."

Do blanch. More is to come on this subject later.

Use the moisture-vapor proof wrapping, or container most suitable, remembering that round containers take up more space than do square ones.

Label each package as to contents, date of freezing and number of servings. This helps you to use up your foods before they stay too long in the freezer. Also, it keeps you from opening a precious package of strawberries when you intended to get out green beans.

Always remember that food must be frozen and stored at 0°F. or lower. One source says that 5°F. below zero gives a good safety factor.

How to freeze will depend on your freezer design. If it is the wrap-around type, you will need to place the packages against the side walls. If you have freezer plate shelves, or a fast-freezing compartment, place the packages in a single layer there. Allow an inch or so between packages for air circulation. If your freezer is at the proper temperature, food will be frozen in about 24 hours and the packages can then be moved into your storage area.

Try not to overload the freezer with too many items to be frozen at one time. This raises the temperature and the cost. A ten cubic foot freezer can't handle more than about 35 pounds of unfrozen food in one day. That's enough for you to process too!

You will want to keep a simple check list, or running inventory of your freezer contents. This is like filling in the stubs of your checkbook. It keeps your food items from getting "lost" and staying overtime, and gives you a chance to space out the family's favorites so that they're not all used up too quickly.

A simple tally like this will be sufficient:

Food	Date Packaged	Size	No. Frozen	No. Used
Peaches	8/1-8/5/72	pints	20	~~1111~~ 1
Peas	6/25-6/29/72	pints	32	~~1111~~ ~~1111~~ 1

It is good management to keep your food groups organized in the freezer. Pawing over a lot of frozen packages looking for the last pint of strawberries you know is there can be very chilly drudgery. If it's in the "fruit corner," you'll find it easily.

Frozen foods are highly perishable after they are thawed and will spoil more quickly than fresh foods. They should be used as soon as possible. Don't overcook your frozen vegetables. Remember that the blanching time is part of the cooking time.

Finally, not a "rule," but a cheerful comment: processing vegetables and fruits for freezing takes about one-third to one-half the time required for canning.

If you expected to read among the basic rules very much on the subject of blanching and packaging, I'll explain that much information was deliberately omitted there. This is because they are such important subjects that they are going to get whole sections to themselves.

PACKAGE IT RIGHT OR YOU'LL BE SORRY I'm going to start right in with a warning. Improper wrapping is the cause of 85 per cent of failure in freezing. Purchasing materials in which to freeze your produce is no place to skimp; nor is the manner in which you seal up the packages. You see, you can't "try out" packaging materials for your freezer as you'd try out a new typewriter or car. Once you put your produce away in the freezer, you're committed to whatever the result is in quality. You may never even know if you've had a large vitamin loss. You will certainly know if the product is tasteless. But by then it's too late. So beware of cheap materials, and do read the manufacturer's labels.

Unless your containers are moisture-vapor proof and

strong, *dehydration* will occur. This simply means that the cold will draw out the moisture from your product, leaving it dry and tasteless. *Oxidation* can be another problem, meaning that oxygen will invade your food and steal away the vitamins. So, you must make certain of the "barrier" to these two forces by using containers which are strong and effectively moisture-vapor proof. Containers which crack easily are a poor buy.

Another thing to watch for in purchasing containers is the ease with which they can be filled or emptied. And do they stack well? To repeat an earlier remark: round containers obviously take up more space than square or rectangular shapes.

Waxed containers, such as milk cartons, will crack at 0°F, although the cracks may be so minute that you can't see them. Coffee cans are great for all kinds of food storage, as are other cans, but they must be lined with some kind of moisture-proof paper to prevent rusting. Also, in the use of coffee cans it is almost impossible to ever get rid of the coffee odor and flavor, so that lining them carefully is a real necessity.

Glass jars may be used, and many people do use them. However, they must be handled very carefully when frozen, as they will break easily. If you do want to use glass containers, be sure to choose those with straight sides; do not choose "shouldered" jars, such as small-mouthed mayonnaise jars. One experience of getting frozen food out of a shouldered jar will burn itself into your memory forever. And do leave head space.

There are many good strong bags on the market suitable for use in freezing. These are made of plastic, or paper that is lined with cellophane, glassine or plastic. Twisted at the top and secured with those bits of wire covered with paper that I call "twists," makes them very useful for some items. I use them myself for such things as frozen green pepper slices, as it's so easy to open the bag, take out the few I want, re-close the bag, and pop it back into the freezer. Two warnings here: 1) these bags can be punctured rather easily, thus permitting dehydration and oxidization, and 2)

unless you have the patience of a saint and strong
fingernails, don't close the bags with rubber bands.
Many homemakers save bread wrappers to use for
storage bags. I have used them myself, but as they are
rather fragile I wouldn't use one more than once, and
then only for short-time freezing and storage.

One great advantage of a strong plastic bag is that,
if not punctured (test by filling it with water), it can
easily be washed out, dried and re-used.

As for containers, the market is flooded with types.
You will find oblong, square, or round paperboard containers lined with glassine, cellophane or wax-impreg-
nated paper. You will probably like the trunk-type used
by so many commercial packers as they are easy to fill,
close, or open.

There are waxy cartons with cardboard or plastic
lids. There are rigid plastic boxes with flexible lids and
flexible plastic boxes with rigid lids.

I think plastic boxes (identified by the maker as
freezer boxes) are a joy forever for vegetables and
fruits. Yes, they understandably cost more than paper,

BAG SEALER Comes with heat sealable bags useful for small portions.
Bags are filled and the open end placed in the slot. Closing the lid forces
the edges together and seals them by heat.

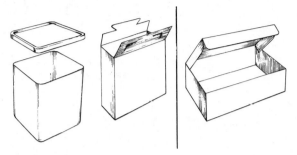

FREEZER CONTAINERS The one on the left is plastic with a snap-on lid and can be used for anything to be frozen. The center and the right ones are made of a plastic coated cardboard and can be re-used but wear out quickly. These should be used in conjunction with plastic bags as liners and the lids closed firmly with freezer tape. All come in ½ pint, pint, quart, and two quart sizes.

but like glass canning jars, are washed after using and stored for the next freezing session, and the next, ad infinitum.

The thing to watch for is the kind of lid that comes with the box. It should not just rest on the top of the box, but should be flexible, snap on, and have an overhang that presses over the container.

You will want to supply yourself with some of the rigid containers I've mentioned to use for carrot fingers and other things that might break when frozen in bags.

Before you purchase any containers, consider the size of your family. Containers should (ideally) be just large enough to accommodate one family meal. In other words, if there are only two of you, the pint and ½-pint sizes will be used most often. In a large family 1½ pint and quart sizes will probably be needed. This suggestion is for economy's sake as every homemaker knows that small amounts of leftovers tend to wind up growing penicillin in the refrigerator.

SHALL WE BLANCH? I can remember when the word "blanching" had the same mysterious ring to me as do the words of a garage mechanic; "Your air filter needs cleaning, lady."

Yes, it's possible to read books and articles on freezing which tell you brightly that blanching is an old, outmoded idea. That just isn't so, and before I tell you how to blanch, I want to tell what it is and why you should do it.

Vegetables and fruits contain enzymes which help to bring about normal ripening. Unless the enzyme action is halted, it continues on to cause over-ripening; changes in flavor, color and texture; and eventually, spoilage. Blanching is a form of partial cooking at high heat which stops the enzymatic action of the product.

It is perfectly true that some vegetables can be frozen without blanching and both look and taste good if eaten within a few months. But for nutritive value, you might as well eat cut-up cardboard. The vitamins have packed up and left.

I am far from being a food faddist, but I do feel that what I eat should do something other than just fill my stomach. I enjoy feeling healthy, and know that this is accomplished by reasonably good nutrition. Also, I like my vitamins in food, not capsules. How about you?

If you don't mind eating vegetables whose color, taste and texture aren't very good, and if nutrition is only a tiresome word to you, go ahead and freeze them without blanching. Your freezer will still be a blessing in convenience, if not in health and nutrition.

Among other things, blanching removes dirt from the pores of the vegetables and destroys almost 100 per cent of the bacteria which may be present. Also, if you're not an organic gardener and have used some chemical sprays these too are washed away to an extent.

Well, that's the "why" of blanching. I don't want to sound dictatorial in telling you how to blanch. It's just that I assume you want to get the most nutritive value out of your vegetables. The world won't fall apart if you over- or under-blanch. Too little blanching may bring about some vitamin loss and color change in the resulting product. Too much blanching may cause you to have a product less crisp and garden-fresh than you might like.

But—if your five-year-old breaks a leg while you're blanching—well there are priorities, aren't there?

A while back I said you'd need a lot of ice for cooling your produce after blanching, and I do mean a lot. The day you freeze vegetables may be hot, and you must rapidly chill several pounds of vegetables which have reached a temperature of 212°F.

The night before you're going to have a freezing session, freeze large blocks of ice in bread tins or saucepans. You will want at least one pound of ice for each pound of vegetables.

Before blanching, prepare your first lot of vegetables as you would for table use, washing them thoroughly and discarding any that are too ripe, too immature, or damaged. Try to sort according to size, for larger vegetables will require more blanching time than smaller ones of the same kind.

There are two methods of blanching: 1) by steam, or 2) in boiling water. A few vegetables may be prepared in other ways, and they will be discussed individually.

Steaming is preferred by some home economists for vegetables that are cut or sliced, as more vitamins and minerals are preserved that way. However, leafy vegetables such as kale, spinach, or similar greens tend to mat together in steaming, and thus, boiling is always recommended for them.

Blanching in boiling water for all vegetables is favored by many authorities despite the greater loss of nutritives than with steaming. This is because in boiling it is easier to be certain of uniform blanching. Well, I've given you two contradictory opinions held by authorities. You'll have to make your own choices.

For steaming, you may use a pressure cooker with a rack, or trivet that has legs long enough to clear completely two inches of boiling water in the bottom of the pan. See Fig. 16 on page 63. Bring the water to a boil, put one layer of vegetables in the basket, and lower it onto the steaming rack. Close lid tightly. If you do use a pressure cooker, don't close the petcock or clamp the lid down, as no steam pressure is required. Start counting the steaming time as soon as the lid is on. If you don't have a pressure cooker, use an ordinary kettle with a snug-fitting lid, and a rack that will keep the steaming basket at least three inches above the bottom of the kettle.

The times necessary for blanching are specified later as the individual vegetables are discussed.

N. B. If you live where you are 5,000 feet or more above sea level, add one minute to the times required for steam blanching.

When the steaming time is finished, the vegetables must be cooled immediately and thoroughly in a large quantity of ice water. The time required for thorough cooling is as much as, or more than, was required for blanching.

Then, drain well, package immediately, label and put in the freezer.

For blanching by boiling use a pot (aluminum or enamel; not iron or copper) big enough to hold at least two gallons of water. See Fig. 18 on page 66. It should have a well-fitting lid and be the kind into which you can fit a mesh wire basket, or strainer with handles. There are special blanching pots on the market, which are very nice to have, but you can make do with the large kettle and strainer quite easily.

Start the water to boil before you begin your vegetable preparation. Speed is of the essence now. It is best to blanch only about a pound of vegetables (two cups) at a time, although with small vegetables such as peas or beans, you may increase this to two pounds. Allow at least one gallon of water for each pound of vegetables.

After preparing the vegetables, as for steam blanching, put them in the basket which is already in the pot of boiling water. If the water is boiling hard, the addition of the small amount of vegetables will not disturb the boiling very long. Keep the heat on high and cover the pot tightly. If you have followed the pound-per-gallon measure, start counting the blanching time when you cover the pot. If the water quiets down after you've put in the vegetables, wait until boil-bubbles appear; then cover and start your timing as given for different vegetables.

N. B. If you live where you are 5,000 feet or more above sea level, add one minute to the times required for boiling-water blanching.

WHAT TO DO WHEN THE LIGHTS GO OUT First, find the candles. Or are you one of these super-efficient people who always has a gas lantern ready for emergencies? It has never been uncommon for country areas, serviced by small electric companies to have frequent and sometimes protracted power failures. Now, great cities are afflicted occasionally, and authorities tell us that this is going to happen more and more frequently. So, we're going to tell all of you what to do about your freezer when this happens.

Don't panic, because you may have several things to do, (such as figuring out how you're going to cook the next meal if you have an electric stove).

The first thing to do, if at all possible, is to find out how long you're likely to be without power. If this is only for a few hours, no precautions are necessary, except that you should not open your freezer.

If you find that it may be longer than a few hours, bet-

ter start rounding up some dry ice. You should already
know of a local source for this, such as an ice cream deal-
er, or a cold storage warehouse.

The more dry ice you use, the longer food will stay
frozen. Twenty-five pounds of dry ice will keep a ten
cubic foot freezer down to zero for two or three days.
Saw or chop the dry ice into pieces proportionate to the
sizes of storage compartments.

I'm sure you know that dry ice burns and that you
must wear gloves when handling it, but you can't say I
didn't remind you.

If any food is on the freezing shelves, move it into the
storage compartment. Place the dry ice on boards of cardboard on top of the packages, never directly on the
packages.

When the freezer is open for putting in the dry ice, plan
to take out any food you may want to use in the next
day or so. This is because you should not open the freezer
again, except to put in more dry ice, until it has been operating for several hours.

Covering the freezer with heavy blankets or rugs helps
to keep the temperature down, but don't cover the air
vents.

How long food will stay frozen depends on several
things:

1. How much food you have in the freezer; a full
   freezer will keep cold much longer than one ‚only
   half full.
2. Temperature of the freezer; the colder it is, the
   longer food will stay frozen. Remember I mentioned that 5°F. below zero gives a safety factor?
3. The freezer itself: i.e., how much insulation it has.
4. The size of the freezer; the larger it is, the longer
   food will stay frozen.

Power failures can happen while you're away from
home, which can be sad if you've left a freezer full of
goodies. It is wise to have a neighbor alerted to take the
measures mentioned above, as well as to make sure to push
the restart switch if the freezer doesn't start running
when the power comes on.

Another nasty little problem can arise. Friends of mine were away for a winter vacation, and the cleaning woman accidentally removed the freezer plug from the electric socket. I'll spare you the details of what the freezer contents looked and smelled like a few weeks later. But I do want you to know that at your local hardware store you can purchase a gadget which will prevent any plug's being removed from a socket unintentionally.

DID IT THAW? Maybe, despite all your best efforts, you think some of your food thawed during the power failure. Don't just stand there wringing your hands; you have too much to do!

As for your fruits, you are in quite a safe position. If they are only partially thawed (i.e., if you can still see a lot of ice crystals in them) they may be re-frozen with a clear conscience—no, I mean with your freezer. If they are completely, or nearly, thawed and don't smell right (fruit can ferment), I'm sorry, but it's spoiled and must be thrown out.

However, if it's completely thawed and is not fermented, you can be very busy making jams, jellies and preserves; pies too.

Vegetables are quite something else. If there are still a lot of ice crystals present, vegetables may be re-frozen, but you may lose quality. You should mark those packages which have been re-frozen. But I'm going to emphasize this: WHEN IN ANY DOUBT about thawed frozen food, never refreeze, and don't eat it yourself or feed it to animals. It could be dangerous.

Bacteria multiply rapidly in vegetables, even at 40°F. On top of having had a freezer problem, you don't want the whole family to be sick.

So, while you're crying a lot—throw it out.

YIELD Before you start any freezing—indeed, maybe before you plant your garden—you'll want to know about how many pints or quarts of frozen vegetables and fruits you can plan on from fresh produce, so here's a table to help you figure it out.

TABLE 8

APPROXIMATE YIELD OF FROZEN VEGETABLES FROM FRESH

Vegetable	Fresh	Frozen
Asparagus	1 crate (12 2-lb. bunches) 1 to 1½ lb.	15-22 pts. 1 pt.
Beans Lima (in pods)	1 bu. (32 lbs.) 2-2½ lbs.)	12-16 pts. 1 pt.
snap (green and wax)	1 bu. (30 lbs.) 2/3-1 lb.	30-45 pts. 1 pt.
soy (in pod)	1 bu. (30 lbs.) 2-2½ lb.	12-15 pts. 1 pt.
Beet greens	15 lb. 1-1½ lb.	10-15 pts. 1 pt.
Beets (without tops)	1 bu. (52 lbs.) 1¼-1½ lb.	35-42 pts. 1 pt.
Broccoli	1 crate (25 lbs.) 1 lb.	24 pts. 1 pt.
Brussels sprouts	4 quarts 1 lb.	6 pts. 1 pt.
Cabbage	small head	1 pt.
Carrots (without tops)	1 bu. (50 lbs.) 1¼-1½ lb.	32-40 pts. 1 pt.
Cauliflower	2 med. heads 1 1/3 lb.	3 pts. 1 pt.
Celery	2 med. bunches	1 pt.
Chard	1 bu. (12 lbs.) 1-1½ lb.	8-12 pts. 1 pt.
Collard greens	1 bu. (12 lbs.) 1-1½ lb.	8-12 pts. 1 pt.
Corn (in husks)	1 bu. (35 lbs.) 2-2½ lb.	14-17 pts. 1 pt.
Eggplant	1 lb.	1 pt.
Kale	1 bu. (18 lbs.) 1-1½ lb.	12-18 pts. 1 pt.
Mustard greens	1 bu. (12 lbs.) 1-1½ lb.	8-12 pts. 1 pt.
Okra	1 lb.	1 pt.
Peas	1 bu. (30 lbs.) 2-2½ lb.	12-15 pts. 1 pt.
Peppers (green)	2/3 lb.	1 pt.
Pumpkin	3 lbs.	2 pts.
Spinach	1 bu. (18 lbs.)	12-18 pts.

Table 8 (Cont.)

Vegetable	Fresh	Frozen
Squash, summer	1 bu. (40 lbs.) 1-1¼ lb.	32-40 pts. 1 pt.
Squash, winter	3 lbs.	2 pts.
Sweet potatoes	2/3 lb.	1 pt.

APPROXIMATE YIELD OF FROZEN FRUITS FROM FRESH

	Fresh	Frozen
Apples	1 bu. 1½ lb.	32-40 pts. 1 pt.
Apricots	1 bu. 2/3 lb.	60-72 pts. 1 pt.
Berries	24 qts. 1½ pt.	32-36 pts. 1 pt.
Cherries, sweet or sour	1 bu. 1½ lb.	36-44 pts. 1 pt.
Cranberries	1 peck 1 lb.	50 pts. 1 pt.
Peaches	1 bu. 1½ lb.	32-48 pts. 1 pt.
Rhubarb	15 lbs. 1 lb.	15-22 pts. 1 pt.
Strawberries	24 qts. 2/3 qt.	38 pts. 1 pt.

"...A tale so free from every doubt—
All probable, possible shadow of doubt..."
THE GONDOLIERS

Seven
FREEZING VEGETABLES AND FRUITS

If I add up all my sources of information, I find that practically anything can be frozen except lettuce. But you will want to experiment with the freezing of various items according to your family's preferences. Also, your available freezer space must be considered. This last is an important consideration.

You will want to organize your thinking ahead of time in order to have a variety of frozen produce and not half-fill your freezer with that early crop of peas! Well, you get the idea.

ARTICHOKES I've never learned to like them (along with beets and sauerkraut), but a great many people do, and I can tell you how to freeze them.

The best varieties for this process grow on the coast of California. Choose those whose leaves are not yet open. First, remove and discard the outermost leaves, then trim the stalk to one inch. With a very sharp knife, cut across the vegetable to expose the layers of tightly packed inner leaves. Blanch, in boiling water, six at a time: three minutes for small artichokes and four for medium-sized ones. Don't bother to freeze the large ones.

After thorough cooling in ice water, drain them upside down on paper towels. Wrap each one in cellophane, sealing with freezer tape, and put enough for a family meal in a large plastic bag or other container.

ASPARAGUS Now *there's* a vegetable. The season is short here in Vermont and in our house we have fresh asparagus for dinner almost every night in May and June. But we freeze some for later enjoyment.

First, break (don't cut) off the bottom woody portion. I bend the stalk with both hands and let it break where it

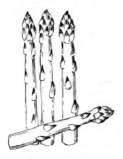

will naturally. Then bunch the asparagus together and cut into even stalks about 5-6″ long. If you have left over pieces, they can be used in salads and soup. Wash the stalks thoroughly, perhaps even removing the little scales from the stalks, because sand hides in there. Sort the spears in three sizes, small, medium and large, by comparing the butt ends.

If you blanch in water, the large spears should boil four minutes, the medium ones three, and the small ones two. If you blanch with steam, tie uniform sizes of the vegetable loosely with string and stand them, heads up, on the rack. Add one minute to the times given for water blanching.

Cool immediately and drain. After this, you can mix up the sizes again if you choose and package in any of several ways: trunk-opening boxes, tall plastic boxes, or even in bags.

BEANS, LIMA You can freeze both large and baby Limas. Both of them should be picked when only about five or ten per cent of the beans have changed from green to white. White Limas are indicative of high starch content; this makes them taste pasty.

When preparing, you will of course, shell and sort them for size. If you want to freeze them in as nearly perfect condition as possible, you can give them the brine-flotation test. This is done by dissolving two cups of salt in 2½ gallons of water that is about 70°F. Add to this solution, about two pounds at a time, the shelled, washed beans. Stir and allow the beans to settle, skimming off the floaters or those suspended in the solution.

The floaters and the swimmers are the perfect beans for freezing. Wash them again, discarding off-color or split beans, before blanching. Any beans which look O.K., but still don't float or swim are not to be discarded by any means. They may be cooked for immediate use, or frozen and labelled "second quality," so that you can compare them with your top quality frozen Limas.

When blanching in water the large ones should be done four minutes, the medium ones three, and small ones two. If blanching in steam, add one minute to each of the above times.

Cool, drain and pack in your favorite containers; but if you choose rigid containers, allow about ½-inch expansion space at the top.

BEANS, SNAP OR WAX   These beans should be harvested for freezing before much development within the pods, because the fibrous material of pods increases with maturity. You will get a better product if the pods are under five inches long.

Wash thoroughly, remove stem ends and any strings. You may leave them whole, cut into pieces, or cut into French-style strips.

Blanching in water will take three minutes for whole beans and two minutes for cut ones. French-style will require only one minute. For blanching by steam, add one minute to the above times.

This is one of the vegetables which requires speedy and very complete cooling. Drain on towels. Pack as you choose, but in rigid containers leave ½-inch head space.

BEANS, SOY   Luckily, this excellent protein food freezes well. Harvest when the pods are plump, bright green and firm. Wash the pods carefully and put them into vigorously boiling water to cook for five minutes. That's all, girls; no more blanching!

Cool pods rapidly in ice water; then, squeeze the beans out of the pods and pack them immediately in any containers. In rigid containers leave ½-inch head space.

BEETS   Beets need to be cooked before freezing, which will no doubt tend to make you choose rather small ones which can be frozen whole. Large beets, sliced for freezing, tend to become rubbery after a few months.

Wash the beets well and sort according to size. Trim off tops and save them! Do not cut, or slice beets at this time. Cook them in boiling water until tender. If they vary in size, put in the largest ones first and add others of graduated sizes at approximately ten-minute intervals.

When beets are tender, cool rapidly under running water. Peel, or rub off skins of mature beets before slicing or dicing them. Whole young beets, no larger than an inch in diameter, may be frozen whole without peeling. Cut beets should be packed in rigid containers, leaving ½-inch head space. Whole beets may be packed in bags, or any flexible containers.

BEET GREENS Now you see why you saved the beet tops. Choose the most tender leaves, removing any tough stems or imperfect parts. Wash very thoroughly. Leave whole, or chop as you choose. Please blanch only in boiling water for two minutes. Steam blanching makes greens mat together.

Cool immediately in ice water, and drain as well as you can on towels. Whole leaves may be packed in bags, but chopped ones should go in rigid containers, leaving ½-inch head space.

BROCCOLI For freezing, select only young shoots with stems not more than an inch thick. Trim off large outer leaves and the woody part of the stems. Wash. Broccoli harbors insects and you'd better be sure you get rid of them by soaking the stalks in a salt solution for a half hour. Use one teaspoon of salt to each quart of water. After this, wash broccoli again to remove saltiness.

Cut pieces lengthwise, trying to make them as uniform as possible, leaving the heads only about 1½ inches across. This assures even blanching.

For blanching in boiling water, do the stalks with 1½-inch heads three minutes, smaller heads two minutes. For blanching with steam, add one minute to the above times. Cool by plunging the blanching basket into very cold water. Drain on towels.

In packaging, lift the stalks with care (using kitchen tongs if you have them), and pack in bags or rigid containers, placing the heads in alternate directions.

BRUSSELS SPROUTS The best sprouts to freeze are dark green in color and not larger than two inches in diameter.

Cut off stems and trim off any wilted or tough leaves. Sort according to size; large, medium and small, and wash thoroughly. If you suspect them of harboring insects, as in broccoli, give them the same salt water soak recommended for that vegetable.

For blanching in boiling water, give the large heads five minutes, medium ones four minutes and small ones three minutes. Add one minute to the above times for blanching in steam.

Cool quickly in ice water, and drain almost dry. Pack closely in the containers of your choice. Brussels sprouts do not expand, so do not need head space if they have been well drained.

CABBAGE Few people freeze cabbage as an economy measure, since there are other ways to store it well, and it takes up freezer space. However, it is perfectly possible to freeze it, and you may want to try some. Do use young cabbage. Trim off tough outer leaves and then separate the head into leaves, or cut it into wedges, or shred it.

Blanch wedges in boiling water three minutes, leaves for two minutes and shreds, 1½ minutes. For blanching in steam add one minute to the above times.

Cool in ice water and drain well. Pack shreds or leaves in bags, but put wedges in rigid containers leaving 1½-inch head space.

CARROTS   The best carrots for freezing are small, young and tender. You can freeze the very large carrots you have toward the end of the season, but why not put those in your root cellar, or cut them up for stews and can them?

Leave the small carrots whole, washing carefully, but not scraping. This last would cause them to lose nutrients. If you have larger carrots you want to freeze, cut them into finger-length halves, or ½-inch round slices.

For blanching in boiling water, the tiny whole carrots need 3½ minutes, the "fingers" three minutes, and the slices two. For steam blanching add two minutes to each of the above times.

Cool rapidly in ice water and drain well. Pack whole carrots or fingers in rigid containers leaving ½-inch head space. Slices may be popped into bags.

For those of you who like the mixture of carrots and peas, they must each be prepared and blanched separately; due to differing time requirements. Then they may be packaged and frozen together, preferably in rigid containers.

CAULIFLOWER   This vegetable takes to freezing better than most; so if it's a family favorite, do plan on some.

Prepare it by cutting the stem close to the head and breaking the head (or cutting it) into flowerets about one inch across. Wash carefully, and if you suspect there are insects present, give it the salt soaking recommended for broccoli. Wash again to remove saltiness and drain.

White cauliflower needs to be bleached (not with Clorox, silly), to keep it from darkening, so steam blanching won't work for this vegetable, unless it's the purple kind. To a gallon of boiling water add the juice of one lemon.

Pieces of cauliflower no larger than an inch need to be blanched only three minutes in this solution, but larger pieces need four minutes.

Pieces of purple cauliflower need one minute more than above times for steam blanching.

If you've never blanched or cooked purple cauliflower before, don't faint when it turns green. That's perfectly normal.

CELERY   No, this delicious vegetable can't yet be frozen raw, although I'm sure that people who study that sort of thing for commercial packers will come up with a method some day. In the meantime, there is no way to store fresh celery, even in common storage, for many months, and it gets very expensive in the stores in the late winter.

So, it's a good idea to grow plenty and freeze some cooked, to be served as a vegetable in winter, with maybe a cheese sauce, or to impart that inimitable flavor to stews and soups.

In preparing it, choose the crispest, most tender stalks. Scrub them well and cut into one-inch pieces. Blanch in boiling water three minutes, or in steam for four. Cool rapidly in ice water.

You may drain and pack dry in bags, or perhaps you will want to pack it in rigid containers with some of the blanching water, leaving ½-inch head space. The latter method is good for any celery to be used for soups, as the liquid can be used also.

COLLARD GREENS   Choose young, tender leaves and prepare them as for beet greens. Blanch in boiling water for three minutes, but not in steam. Remember? Steam blanching makes greens mat together. Package as was recommended for beet greens.

CORN I doubt if you could get any group of women together, all experienced in freezing corn, who would agree
on the "best" method. I'll just have to tell you about
methods I've found out about and from then on you're on
your own. By the way, all methods mentioned are tried
and tested. I'll be willing to bet I'll hear from people
who have still other methods not yet known to me.

The first thing to remember is that, especially for corn,
the final cooking procedures are as vital as are the freezing
procedures.

The second thing to be considered right now while
you're thinking about freezing, is the matter of space. I'm
sure you'll want to try varying methods of freezing corn,
but you'll be surprised at how much freezer space the
whole cobs take.

Be certain that your corn is exactly ripe. To do this, strip
down a piece of husk and pierce a kernel with your thumbnail. If milk spurts, the corn is prime for freezing. The ears
should be fully developed.

Method 1

Husk ears quickly, remove all silk and wash ears under running water. Put aside ears with shrunken or under-
sized kernels. They can be used for cream-style packaging. Sort ears according to length and diameter.

For boiling water blanching do large ears about seven
minutes, medium ears five minutes and small ones three or
four minutes. If blanching with steam, add one minute to
the above times.

Cool speedily in ice water and wipe each ear dry. Wrap
each ear separately in cellophane or freezer paper and
freeze. Then, when frozen, the wrapped ears may be consolidated into bags for easier storage.

Method 2

If you want to be extravagant about using aluminum
foil, after husking the corn, wrap each ear carefully in
heavy-weight foil. Drop the ears into boiling water and
add one minute to the blanching times given in Method 1.
Then plunge corn into plenty of ice water and chill for
double the blanching time.

To serve corn packaged and frozen in this way, simply remove from the freezer and drop it into cold water which you bring to the boiling point. Remove from water, unwrap and serve.

Method 3

I am told that you can freeze corn in the husk, but that it should not be left in the freezer for more than two months. You do it this way: do not disturb the husks at all, but bend the silk back onto the husks and secure tightly with a string or wire twist. Put corn in direct contact with freezer coil, or on the coldest freezer shelf.

When ears are solidly frozen you may package several together for easier storage.

Corn frozen in this way should be thawed in cold water before husking. Boil until tender, or roast un-husked ears in a moderately hot oven. If you use this roasting method, put a pan with about ½-inch of water in it on the bottom oven shelf.

Method 4

This is corn sans cob. One of my friends who has a beautiful garden, a gourmet appetite (and is a gourmet cook to boot) swears by this method, and she's tried them all. She cooks corn completely as for the table; and when it's cool enough to handle, she cuts off the kernels, pops them into meal-size containers and freezes them. She's done this for two years now and says that after thawing, when heated with butter, salt and pepper, all you lack for the fun and good taste of having fresh corn is chewing it from the cob.

CORN, CREAM STYLE If you're like most gardeners, you have several ears of corn which are less than perfect, and this method of storing them serves a useful purpose. Follow instructions as given for corn on the cob in Method 1, until ready to blanch. Then blanch large ears in boiling water for four minutes. Cool rapidly in ice water. With a sharp knife cut corn from the cobs about half way through the kernels.

Put the kernels in a bowl; then hold the cobs over the

bowl and with the back of your knife, scrape the cobs to catch the milky juice and kernel hearts.

Stir this well and put in refrigerator to chill. When thoroughly cold, pack the corn in rigid containers, leaving ½-inch head space and freeze.

CORN, WHOLE KERNEL   Follow instructions for cream-style corn, but cut the kernels as close to the cob as you can, without cutting into the cob. When thoroughly chilled, pack in bags, or any containers.

HERBS   Freezing herbs is simple and yields very satisfactory results for chopped herbs—not whole leaves. The method is easy. When you gather a handful of any herb, wash and pat dry. No blanching. It is best not to chop them at this time as the chopping produces some oxidation. The frozen leaves will not be suitable for garnishes, but mincing them on a chopping board for seasoning is easy.

Store the washed dry herbs in plastic sandwich bags, or any small containers you have handy that can be well-sealed. Close tightly, label and freeze.

All herbs may be frozen, but I know you will find that those of delicate flavor such as chives, mint or tarragon keep their true flavor better than in the drying process.

Some mixtures of herbs for certain foods are traditional:

i.e., *fines herbes*. Rather than take a sprig of chervil, chives, sweet marjoram and parsley from each of four containers when I'm making *omelette aux fines herbes*, I freeze some envelopes of them together, so that I only open one envelope for the omelette.

Dill leaves can be frozen to chop to use in potato salads or fish chowders. Frozen mint makes excellent mint sauce. And so on. You're limited only by the amount of herbs you've grown and by your imagination. It's all a much cheaper trick than buying those expensive jars of dried herbs at your grocer's.

KALE The best kale for freezing is tightly curled and picked when young and tender. It is important with this vegetable to work with very small amounts at a time (a pound or two), in order to retain its high nutritive content. The remainder that you want to freeze that day should be kept unwashed in plastic bags in the vegetable crisper of your refrigerator.

Wash the kale you're going to blanch; and this must be done thoroughly under running water. Pull leaves from the stems and blanch in boiling water for one minute. Kale, like all greens, should not be steamed. Cool thoroughly, and if you wish to chop the kale, it may be done at this time.

Package whole leaves in bags; but chopped kale should be packed in rigid containers, leaving ½-inch head space.

OKRA This vegetable, which never grows up North where I live, is famous in warmer climates, especially for use in soups.

For freezing select young tender pods. Remove stems, but don't cut into the seedy parts, or slice it before blanching.

Blanch in boiling water thus: large pods three minutes, medium pods two minutes and small, one minute. If you blanch in steam, add one minute to the above times.

Cool well in ice water and drain on towels. At this time you can, if desired, cut okra into slices ½-inch thick.

Pack whole pods in bags, or slices in rigid containers leaving ½-inch head space.

MUSTARD GREENS Follow the directions given for kale.

PEAS Everyone with a freezer wants to freeze this delicious vegetable, but the result is not always what the homemaker expected. This, according to research authorities in the frozen food industry, is because people often attempt to freeze peas that are too mature. One extra day on the vine can make peas too starchy for best flavor. So, do harvest your peas before they are quite mature. Also, before packaging them for freezing, you can give them the brine flotation test described for Lima beans. The only difference is that for peas you should use two cups of salt and only one gallon of water. Thus you can freeze "first and "second" quality peas and compare the results.

For easy shelling of peas, plunge pods in boiling water for one minute, then cool immediately in ice water. The peas can be squeezed out of the pods in no time at all.

Discard any hard or damaged peas. Blanch in boiling water as steam blanching of peas does not always give uniform results. Boil for one minute if you shelled them raw, but only a half minute if you boiled the pods before shelling the peas.

Lift your strainer or basket in and out of the water to distribute the heat evenly over the peas. Then, dunk the basket directly in ice water. Drain the peas until they are dry. Pack in rigid containers leaving ½-inch head space.

PEPPERS, GREEN BELL Not everyone would agree with me, but I can't imagine a freezer without peppers in it. For one reason, they are so darned expensive in the stores in the winter; and also, there's really no other way to store this vegetable successfully for more than a few weeks. They can be frozen in such ways as to provide a nice number of uses.

You can freeze halves to have them ready for stuffing, in strips for all those dishes you make that call for "sautéed green pepper," or in thinly sliced rings for salads.

For freezing halves, choose peppers which have no blemishes; cut off caps, and cut peppers in half lengthwise. Remove the seeds and ribs. Wash well and blanch in boiling water for three minutes. Cool quickly and drain. The halves are most easily packaged in bags.

If you slice peppers in thin rings, blanch two minutes and cool; you will want to pack them in rigid containers leaving ½-inch head space. These can be used for your salads in winter. Use when only partially thawed, so they are still crisp.

Save any blemished peppers for slicing in strips, as it will be easy to cut out the blemishes. Then blanch two minutes and cool quickly. I put these, chopped or unchopped, in bags with wire twists for easy access. It's simple to open the bag, take out the amount needed for cooking, and pop the rest back into the freezer.

POTATOES, SWEET These must be cooked before freezing. Scrub them thoroughly and cook by boiling or baking until they are nearly tender. Let them stand at room temperature until cool, then peel. Leave small potatoes whole, but cut larger ones into halves or slices.

To prevent the potatoes from darkening, dip them into a quart of water to which you've added ½ cup of lemon juice. Leave potatoes in this liquid for about five seconds, making sure they are covered with the liquid. Drain potatoes on towels and package in bags or boxes just as they are. Or, you can roll them in brown sugar first to have them ready for candying.

You may wish to freeze mashed sweet potatoes, in which case, allow the vegetable to cook until completely tender. Scoop out from the skins and mash thoroughly, adding about two tablespoons of lemon or orange juice to each quart of potatoes. These should be packed in rigid containers leaving ½-inch head space.

POTATOES, WHITE BAKED STUFFED   Unless you're a strictly utilitarian cook, there's something luxurious about knowing you have baked stuffed potatoes tucked away in your freezer for those special meals.

You only have to bake them thoroughly, remove pulp from the shells and cool at room temperature. Put pulp back in shells. Then wrap individually in foil, freezer paper, or cellophane and freeze. After freezing, they may be consolidated into bags for easier storage. Before reheating, they can be topped with cheese, or any gourmet touch you fancy.

PUMPKIN   If you wish to serve pumpkin as a vegetable, prepare it as you would for the table—removing seeds, then baking, steaming, or boiling—then removing the pulp and mashing it while it's hot. Cool it by putting a bowlful into cold water and stirring it occasionally. When it's cold, pack in rigid containers leaving ½-inch head space.

If your family likes pumpkin pie, you can probably make a lot of Brownie points by freezing pumpkin pie mix. Prepare as you usually do, but be sure to use homogenized, pasteurized milk or cream. When cool, package enough for one pie in each rigid container. Or, if you're terribly efficient, put it into unbaked pie shells and freeze the whole thing.

SPINACH   You should choose only very dark green spinach for freezing. As with kale, work with only a pound or two at a time, keeping the balance unwashed and refrigerated.

Remove large stems and any bruised or discolored leaves. Wash, wash and wash. One source we know of uses a washing machine, on the rinse cycle, for degritting spinach.

Pull large leaves apart, or cut them with scissors. Blanch in water only (no steaming), and three gallons is recommended for each pound of spinach. Blanching time is two minutes.

Cool very quickly, and try not to let it mat. Drain as well as possible and pack loosely in bags or rigid containers.

SQUASH, SUMMER AND ZUCCHINI Select small vegetables (say, not more than 8″ long) that have a slightly tender rind. Wash and cut, without peeling, into ½-inch slices. Blanch in water for three minutes, or in steam for four.

Cool quickly in very cold water and drain on towels. Package, without pressing down, in rigid containers leaving ½-inch head space.

SQUASH, WINTER Prepare just as directed for pumpkin. Pack in rigid containers leaving ½-inch head space.

Acorn squash may be prepared and frozen in the same way, but in our house we like it cut into halves and baked with butter until tender. Cool the halves at room temperature, then wrap each half individually and freeze. Later, for easier storage the halves can be consolidated in bags. You can serve the squash as is, when re-heated, or stuffed with pork sausage, sea food, or other vegetables.

SWISS CHARD Prepare exactly as directed for spinach.

TOMATOES A great many people believe that it is impossible to freeze tomatoes, but that is a myth. You can not only freeze tomatoes but, certain freezer conditions being present, you can freeze 'em raw.

For whole cooked tomatoes, choose rather small ones. Wash, remove stems and any blemishes. Put them in a flat pan of boiling water until the skins crack. Remove them with a slotted spoon and let cool until they can be handled. Peel and core them and let them simmer in their own juice until soft, but not falling apart. This will take only about five minutes. Cool at room temperature and then chill in the refrigerator. Pack in rigid containers, with their own juice, leaving ½-inch head space.

You can also freeze raw tomatoes if you have an upright freezer and freezer plate shelves, or a chest type with a fast-freezing compartment.

You should choose the small, almost seedless tomatoes that are harvested early in the season for this process. Handle them with care to prevent bruising, and put them, unwashed, directly on the freezer plate which has been lined with freezer paper; or set them on paper in the fast-freezing compartment of your chest.

When the tomatoes are frozen, you will see that the skin is cracked in several places. It will be easy to remove. Peel, as rapidly as you can, put in bags and back into the freezer. Be sure they're stored in a location where they won't be easily crushed.

Before you plan to use any, remove the required number and let them thaw partially in the refrigerator. When served in salads, they should still be frosty and retain some ice crystals.

You may not care for them. They will never rival the fresh, ripe ones right out of your garden in summer, but they are still a lot better than those half-ripe, tasteless packaged things sold in the store in winter under the name of "tomatoes."

FRUITS AND BERRIES

Well, at least we have a change of subject from blanching, as now we'll be discussing different methods of packing fruits and berries for freezing. Not one of them needs to be blanched! In fact, freezing fruits and berries is among life's simpler occupations, as they require little more preparation than for the table.

There are, of course, a few special rules about the process, and here they are.

Unlike vegetables, many of which are best frozen when not quite mature, fruits and berries should be at their very peak of ripeness. It is unwise to pick more than you believe you can process in one day, as it doesn't improve the product any to stand around waiting for you.

I knew all this, but will never forget my first experience at freezing strawberries. Husband out of town—children too young to stay up and help—and when I finally finished my job at 2:00 A.M., I never wanted to see another strawberry. You can bet I never picked too many at once again, either.

The kind of utensils you use are very important. Iron, copper, or thinly-tinned vessels may produce off-flavors, and do avoid galvanized wear like the plague. The zinc used in its manufacture dissolves in fruit acid juices. So, let us hope you are prepared with enamel, aluminum, or stainless steel ware. Buy, beg or borrow.

As you did for vegetables, you will require a lot of ice for your preparations. Make blocks ahead of time, as previously suggested. You're going to have to wash all the fruits and berries, and ice water firms them up quickly. This prevents sogginess and loss of juice. It also freezes your hands, but if it's a hot day, aren't you lucky?

When draining fruits or berries is called for, use a colander or absorbent towels, taking care not to jostle the products much. They are far more fragile than most vegetables, and need TLC in handling.

Work with only a quart of berries at a time, or two or three quarts of fruit. This is because you must work with great speed, and a small amount gives you the opportunity to do so.

The packaging materials you use for fruits and berries must be firm, vapor-proof and absolutely leak-proof. Some fruit juices are so acid they will eat right through poorly treated paper or cardboard. Wasted food and Operation Mess!

Glass jars (not shouldered) or well-waxed cardboard tubs are both excellent, as are those handy plastic ice cream or artificial whipped cream containers you've been saving.

As with vegetables, it's most practical to pack only as much fruit in a container as can be used at once. For example, one quart of berries gives four generous servings as a dessert; a pint will yield sauce for four. A quart of fruit makes a nine-inch pie.

With all berries you should rush each package into the freezer as soon as it is sealed. Don't wait until you have them all done.

Do remember that freezing performs no magic, and your end product will be no better than what you chose to freeze.

SOME FRUITS TURN DARK—NOW WHAT? You know all about how quickly bananas, peaches and some other fruits will turn dark when they are peeled. They then look very unappetizing. It turns out that chemists, in investigating the private lives of fruits, discovered some tiny compounds which are now named catechols and tannins. These compounds are colorless so long as they are protected from oxygen by the peel of the fruit. The instant they are exposed to air they become colored and the result is darkened fruit which soon loses its aroma and flavor: air has oxidized it.

While catechols and tannins are present, in varying degrees, in all fruits and berries, you've noticed that citrus fruits retain their color well when peeled. This is because of the different content of vitamin C in each of the fruits. Vitamin C is ascorbic acid, which forms a natural barrier to air oxidization of the fruit. The more ascorbic acid in a fruit, the slower the oxidization process. Another compound in citrus fruits is citric acid which aids in preventing oxidization.

These chemical life processes of fruits explain why, when you are freezing them, you must work as rapidly as possible. It also explains the advisability of adding ascorbic-citric acid to the syrup when freezing the fruits which darken easily.

There are several such preparations on the market, but it is wise to buy only those prepared by reputable pure food or drug companies. Follow the manufacturer's directions.

FOUR KINDS OF PACKS There are four acceptable methods of packing fruits and berries, as follows:

Unsweetened Dry Pack

This method is primarily useful for fruits or berries which are intended for pies, jams or preserves at a later time. I often do this in the summer, when very busy with fresh garden produce, then make jams and preserves in the fall when things quiet down.

The method is also good for people on special diets which restrict sugar.

The procedure is to wash (in ice water) the fruit or berries in a colander and pack immediately in rigid containers. Seal and freeze. When you label the container, it's a good idea to add "Dry, unsweetened," to the other information in the labeling.

Unsweetened Wet Pack

This method is useful for any fruits or berries that are already sweet enough, or again, for people on restricted diets.

The procedure is to pack the product (after washing in ice water and draining) in liquid-proof containers. You may crush it gently in its own juice, or cover with water that has an ascorbic-citric acid solution. Allow ½-inch head space. Label package completely, seal and freeze.

Dry Sugar Pack

This pack is especially useful for fruits or berries that you intend to use for pies because there is much less liquid.

There are two procedures for this pack, one with and one without ascorbic-citric acid.

For peaches or other fruits which darken quickly you'll want to use ascorbic-citric acid for the reasons mentioned in the section on that subject. Prepare the fruit as for the table. Treat sugar by mixing well three teaspoons of the ascorbic-citric acid powder with each two cups of sugar used. Sprinkle treated sugar on the bottom of the container then fill the container a quarter full of fruit. Sprinkle more treated sugar. Fill container to the half-way mark and repeat sugar treatment. Continue with this alternating procedure until container is filled within a half-inch of the top; finish with another sprinkling of sugar. Seal, label and freeze.

The other procedure is for berries which almost never require the ascorbic-citric acid, or for any fruits which do not discolor. Prepare product as for the table. Put in a bowl (working with one quart or less at a time) and sprinkle in the amount of sugar recommended for each fruit. Using a slotted spoon, lift fruit gently until it is evenly coated with the sugar. Continue mixing gently until fruit juices are drawn out and sugar is dissolved. Pack in rigid containers, or bags. Seal, label and freeze.

Syrup Pack

This pack is most often used for fruits or berries that have little juice of their own and for fruits that discolor quickly when exposed to air.

Syrup to use may be made of water and sugar, water and white corn syrup, water and honey, or water and a combination of all three, according to your own desires. One comment directed to those of you who want to avoid refined white sugar: brown sugar may be used if the resulting color doesn't disturb you. For those of you who prefer natural foods and think you could use honey alone for sweetening, here's a warning. Don't, unless you are very fond of honey! It overpowers the flavor of fruits and berries to such an extent that all you can taste is the honey.

Syrups may be thin, medium or heavy, and the one you use will depend on how sour your fruit is and how sweet you want it to be.

SYRUPS FOR FREEZING FRUITS

Sugar Syrup: Use Boiling Water			
Per Cent of Syrup	Cups of Sugar	Cups of Water	Yield: Cups of Syrup
20	1	4	5
30	2	4	5 1/3
40	3 1/2	4	5 1/2
50	4 3/4	4	6 1/2
60	7	4	7 3/4
70	9	4	8 2/3

Dissolve the sugar completely in boiling water, wait until the syrup cools and then store it in the refrigerator until you are ready to cover the fruit for freezing. Whenever possible, a 40 per cent syrup or less is preferred, as heavier syrups tend to make fruits flabby.

Ascorbic-citric acid powder is added to the cold syrup. Follow manufacturer's directions for amount to use for each fruit.

Whenever using corn syrup with sugar use cold water. A thin syrup would require 1 cup sugar, 2 cups corn syrup, 6 cups water and yield 8 cups of syrup.

A medium syrup requires 2 cups sugar, 2 cups corn

syrup, 5 cups water and the yield will be 8 cups of syrup.

A heavy syrup requires 3 cups sugar, 2 cups corn syrup, 4 cups water and yields 8 cups of syrup.

The method for making any of these is to dissolve the sugar first in the measured amount of cold water called for, then add the corn syrup and mix thoroughly. Store in refrigerator until needed.

Honey may be substituted for the corn syrup, if desired, but do remember that both of these may give a foreign flavor to the fruit.

As for the sugar syrups, ascorbic-citric acid is added to the cold corn or honey syrups, according to the manufacturer's directions.

WHICH METHOD FOR YOU?　You have the four choices of the kinds of packs you may use for fruits and berries, which may seem bewildering at first. One way to arrive at a decision is to be guided by your own sweet tooth. Then, how tart is your product, and finally for what purpose(s) will it be used? I have made some general suggestions in the discussion of each method.

I must remind you to allow plenty of head space in packaging fruit. An inch, or inch and a half is not too much for liquid packs. You can keep fruit from rising out of the syrup by crumpling some cellophane over the top before closing the container.

STORAGE TIME　The length of storage time for fruits and berries will vary somewhat. If they are properly prepared and packaged, and given the ascorbic-citric acid treatment when recommended, most raw fruits and berries will keep up to a year at 0°F.

However, if pre-cooked, such as applesauce, they should be used within four months.

INDIVIDUAL METHODS FOR PREPARING FRUITS

APPLES　This fruit may be frozen for various purposes: sliced for pies or other desserts, baked whole, or made into sauce.

If you're going to slice them, it's a good idea to have a pan of very cold water nearby, and drop the peeled, cored apples in there until you have enough to slice. This somewhat retards the fast oxidization of the fruit. You can pack them dry and unsweetened, sweet dry (one cup sugar to three cups of apples) or in a 40 per cent syrup, heated with ascorbic-citric acid.

If you use the syrup pack, slice the apples directly into containers which have some syrup in them. Add syrup as you go along, to keep the apples covered.

When freezing baked apples, bake them as you always do. They can be fast-frozen on the freezer-plate shelf, or in the fast-freezing compartment; then packed in bags.

I like to freeze quite a lot of applesauce to have handy for just re-heating to serve with roast pork and other meals. I do this rather early in the season, using the "drops" which are apt to be blemished and won't store well anyway. There are two schools of thought on applesauce. One would have you cook and strain it to a mush. If you come to dinner at our house, you'll get sauce that is chunky, and the apples weren't peeled. If it worries you to have the sauce turn dark (mine is dark with spices anyway), you can add 1½ teaspoons of ascorbic-citric acid powder to each cup of sugar you use. Pack in rigid containers, leaving one-inch head space. Seal and freeze.

APRICOTS You can freeze them in halves without peeling, or in peeled slices.

For halves, choose fully ripe apricots with smooth yellow skins. Wash under running water, cut into halves and remove pits. If you want to freeze unpeeled halves, dropping them into boiling water for a half-minute will prevent the skins from toughening. Chill immediately in ice water and drain.

A 40 per cent syrup, heated with ascorbic-citric acid, is best for these halves. Put some syrup in the containers, then fruit, and so on, keeping the fruit covered. Leave a one-inch head space, seal and freeze. These can be served as a dessert by themselves, or as a cocktail fruit.

To freeze sliced apricots for pies and so on, drop them whole into boiling water for one minute. Remove and put them into ice water until they are completely cool. You can then skin them easily. Put some 40 per cent syrup, heated with ascorbic-citric acid, into containers and slice the fruit in, doing this alternately, always keeping the fruit covered. Leave a one-inch head space, seal and freeze.

CHERRIES, SOUR This fruit has a short season, and you have to get to the tree before the birds do. Once you have the cherries, fully ripe, firm them in ice water for about an hour. Sort them and remove pits. There is a cherry-pitting gadget on the market, but if you don't have one you can make your own. Straighten out a paper clip and then, with the help of tweezers or pliers, make a small hook at one end. This can be your answer-of-the-day to Conspicuous Consumption. Well, back to the cherries— you probably intend to use them for pies, and a dry sugar pack is best.

For every two quarts of cherries, use 1½ cups sugar, mixing it in well with a wooden spoon until the cherries are well-coated and the sugar dissolved. Pack in glass or rigid plastic containers. It is unwise to use paper or cardboard, as sometimes the acid in the fruit never freezes at all and can eat right through anything but glass or plastic.

CHERRIES, SWEET Be sure these are fully ripe and sweet. Wash under running water (they don't need the ice water treatment recommended for sour cherries). It is a good idea not to pit them, as sweet cherries frozen with their pits will acquire a slight, delicious almond flavor.

If you have a fast-freezing shelf or compartment, you can spread the cherries out on waxed paper and freeze them that way. Then frozen, they can be bagged for storage.

If you don't choose that method, you can put them in containers half full of 40 per cent syrup. Seal and freeze.

CRABAPPLES When these are ripe and ready, you may be too busy to make jelly. You can freeze them as directed for pie apples, until a later time when you are ready for a jelly-making session.

CRANBERRIES   Cranberries are not fragile and may be prepared and packed for freezing in almost any way you choose. They should be firm, well-colored and glossy, with no mealiness. Stem and sort them, discarding any shriveled or soft berries. Wash and drain.

You may freeze them on paper in the fast-freezing area, as suggested for sweet cherries. You can pack them dry and unsweetened in bags or rigid containers. Or, you may want to pack them in containers with a cold 50 per cent syrup.

And why not freeze that incomparable relish you make with cranberries and oranges, that you've put through the food chopper?

Anyway, I want to convince you that cranberries in some form or other taste just as good in May as at Thanksgiving. If you have them frozen, you'll use them to your family's delight.

FRUIT JUICE, APPLE   If you are the proud owner of an electric juicer, or have access to an apple press, why not freeze some apple juice in plastic or glass containers? Add about one teaspoon ascorbic-citric acid to each gallon of juice. Be sure to leave at least one-inch head space in each container.

Cider, or apple juice packed commercially usually has a preservative in it which won't take kindly to freezing.

FRUIT JUICES, CITRUS   Blessedly lucky are those of you who live where you can walk out in your yard and pick your breakfast grapefruit. However, even you can't do this all year 'round, and there's no reason why you shouldn't freeze some juice while the citrus crop is plentiful.

The juiciest fruit will feel heavy for its size. Chill it in ice water before cutting, then cut and remove seeds. Squeeze out the juice, and if you must, strain it. Leaving bits of pulp in makes a more nutritious, tasty product.

Add ¼ teaspoon of ascorbic-citric acid to each quart of juice, but mix this in carefully, so as not to mix in air which would introduce oxygen and defeat the action of the acid.

Pour into glass or rigid plastic containers leaving one-inch head space.

For lemon and lime juice, an easy trick is to freeze it in ice cube trays. When solidly frozen, remove cubes and bag them. They will be handy for flavorings when thawed as needed, or used frozen for iced drinks.

FRUIT JUICES, NON-CITRUS You will nearly always find in any batch of berries or fruits you're preparing for freezing some that are too ripe for a good product. Put them in the refrigerator until your main freezing project is completed, and use them for frozen juices, either as single flavors, or by mixing several together in a tasty blend.

Wash, and remove stems, pits and any bruised portions. Cook in a stainless steel or aluminum pot over low heat, simmering until juice is separated from the pulp. If the fruit is firm and not very juicy, add ½ cup water for every quart of fruit cooking. Do not boil.

When you think you have all the juice you're going to get, remove from stove and cool it at room temperature. Strain it through a cloth jelly bag and sweeten, if necessary. Chill overnight in the refrigerator. Add one teaspoon of ascorbic-citric acid to each gallon of juice. Pour into glass or plastic containers, leaving one-inch head space. Freeze.

GRAPEFRUIT After cutting in half, remove sections without the membrane, saving the juice in another container. To each quart of juice add ½ cup sugar and ¼ teaspoon ascorbic-citric acid powder. Package the fruit in rigid containers, covering it with juice and leaving one-inch head space.

ORANGES This fruit will freeze, pack, and keep better if sliced, rather than sectioned. Peel fully ripe oranges and take off as much membrane as possible. Cut into ¼-inch slices. Pack in rigid containers and cover with orange juice to which has been added ½ teaspoon of ascorbic-citric acid for each quart of juice. Let your sweet tooth be your guide as to the question of adding any sugar. Seal and freeze.

PEACHES Now this is a temperamental fruit to freeze as it oxidizes so quickly, but you can get a good product if you're careful. And oh, that peach shortcake in the middle of the winter!

It is true that giving the peaches a boiling water bath to loosen the skins is often recommended, but it seems safer (and harder) to peel and pit them under cold running water. Do just one at a time, and slice or halve it into a solution of two tablespoons of ascorbic-citric acid to a gallon of ice water. The peaches will want to rise to the top but you can prevent this by putting a heavy plate over the top, then taking it off only to add another peach.

When you have about two quarts of peaches prepared, it's time to pack them. You can lift them out with a slotted spoon into containers which are about a quarter filled with 40 per cent syrup, adding more syrup to cover completely.

Or, you can drain them on absorbent towels, blotting them gently, and then put them into a well-chilled bowl. With a wooden spoon, turn them over in ½ cup sugar until all the fruit is covered. Pack dry in rigid containers. Seal and freeze.

If you've succeeded in keeping the peaches from turning brown in the freezer, there is still another trick to follow about thawing; for as soon as they are thawed and open to the air, they will start turning brown. So, defrost them slowly in your refrigerator and serve when still a little frosty. By the time you are eating them, they'll be just right.

RHUBARB   The early spring crop of young tender rhubarb is your best choice for freezing. You probably want to plan on it for pies next winter, and this is a simple matter.

Wash under cold running water and cut it into preferred lengths. Drain thoroughly and pack it in rigid containers. Seal and freeze.

INDIVIDUAL METHODS FOR PREPARING BERRIES

All berries are about the easiest things to freeze, for they need no ascorbic-citric acid treatment, and you may sweeten them or not, according to your palate and the uses for which you plan them.

And for those of you who have fast-freezing plates, or compartments, here's a tip. As soon as the berries are soaked, washed, and drained, you can put them in a single layer on wax paper in the freezer. They will freeze very quickly, and can then be poured into bags or other containers for storing.

BLACKBERRIES These should be fully ripe, dark and glossy, but not over-mature. After sorting, put about a quart at a time in a colander and move this up and down in ice water, carefully, so that all berries get washed and firmed. Turn them out on absorbent towels and drain almost dry.

If you're going to use them for cooked desserts such as pies, cobblers and so on, they may be packed directly in rigid containers without adding sugar or syrup. Leave one-inch head space, seal and freeze.

BLUEBERRIES Remove all stems and sort carefully, discarding any which are under-ripe. Wash in ice water and drain thoroughly.

The skins of these berries tend to toughen, so it is best to crush them slightly before freezing, with or without any sweetening.

For pies, muffins, or any cooked desserts, pack the berries dry and unsweetened in rigid containers or bags.

For uncooked desserts, pack in a 40 per cent syrup leaving one-inch head space.

Or you can use a dry sugar pack, with ½-¾ cup sugar to four cups of berries. Mix to coat well with sugar. Seal and freeze.

RASPBERRIES Sort out under-ripe, seedy, or over-ripe berries. The seedy and over-ripe ones make great puree or juice. Wash the ones you are going to freeze, about a quart at a time. This should be done carefully in ice water, using a colander as was recommended for blackberries. Drain well. Freeze in direct contact with freezer-plate, if possible. Then, just pop them, frozen, into bags.

You can use a sugar pack if desired, which will take about 2/3 cup sugar to each quart of berries. Make sure all berries are well coated with sugar, then pack in rigid containers leaving a one-inch head space.

If you prefer to use a syrup pack, put berries in rigid containers and cover with a 30-40 per cent syrup, leaving one-inch head space. Seal and freeze.

Now you can wash those very seedy or over-ripe berries for purée. Press them through a sieve or food mill. Add as much sugar as you think it needs, mix until sugar is dissolved. Pack in rigid containers leaving one-inch head space. This purée is delicious as a sauce over ice cream or cake.

STRAWBERRIES   You may wish to freeze some berries whole in dry sugar or syrup pack, but the result may not please you. Why not try a quart or two the first year, and compare them with those which are cut in half or sliced, or even just crushed a little? I believe you will prefer berries which you slice or barely crush.

For any type of pack, select firm, mature berries. Wash in ice water, drain thoroughly, then remove hulls.

For syrup pack, partially fill containers with 40-50 per cent syrup, add berries, and cover with syrup to within an inch of the top. Seal and freeze.

For dry sugar pack, use ½-¾ cup sugar for each quart of fruit. Mix carefully until fruit is coated and sugar dissolved. Pack in rigid containers leaving one-inch head space.

Well, as you've gathered, it's perfectly possible to make your freezer stand up and do tricks if you, too, have "done your thing" in observing the limitations.

Freeze the best possible vegetables and fruits and berries, package them right, and you'll have good, nutritious eating.

"Does your human being inner
Feed on everything that nice is?"
THE GONDOLIERS

Eight
RECIPES

When this book was in the planning stage, even after the writing had begun, no one thought of including any recipes. However, the idea developed as time went on, and I hope you like it. I have chosen some "musts" to add to the collection of recipes you already have. These include some representative ways in which you can serve foods from all the kinds of storage discussed throughout the book.

VEGETABLE RECIPES

ASPARAGUS For years I put a rubber band around asparagus spears (frozen, fresh, or canned), then stood them upright in a kettle to cook or heat through. Only two or three years ago did I read somewhere that preparing asparagus flat in a large skillet would give excellent results. The asparagus should be just barely covered with boiling water. This method is easy, as the vegetable cooks or heats through evenly and without breaking the heads. Don't drain water off asparagus; instead, lift it out gently with spoons or spatulas to the serving dish. For a taste treat, cover with almond-butter sauce. (See Sauces and Other Temptations).

BEANS, BOSTON BAKED For those of us who have grown up in New England, canned baked beans bear not the slightest relationship in flavor to the true Boston baked beans. Yes, the latter take time to make, but you will find it well worthwhile, and here's how you do it. By the way, if you can latch onto one or more of the old-fashioned brown earthenware bean pots, by all means do so. However, there's no law that says you can't bake the beans in casseroles.

Use two pounds of dried kidney, California or pea beans. Wash, discarding any imperfect ones. Cover with two quarts of water; bring to the boiling point; boil two minutes, then let soak one hour or more.

Without draining, cook slowly until the skins burst when you take a few on the tip of a spoon and blow on them. Drain, reserving the cooking water.

Cover ½ pound fat salt pork with boiling water and let stand two minutes; drain and cut one-inch gashes every ½-inch in the pork without cutting through the rind. Put the beans in the pot or casserole. Push the pork down into the beans until all but the rind is covered.

Mix two teaspoons salt, one cup molasses, one teaspoon dry mustard and two tablespoons sugar, (brown or white). Add this mixture to the cup of water reserved from cooking the beans and bring to the boiling point. Pour over the beans and add enough more water to cover them. Cover the pot.

Bake six to eight hours at 250°. Add water, as needed, to keep the beans moist. Uncover during the last hour of baking so that the rind of the pork is brown and crisp. This amount of baked beans will serve ten or more people.

An additional hint is that many people like onion in their baked beans; and you can either put in a few slivers, mixing well with the beans, or a whole, peeled onion which you will remove before serving the beans.

BEANS, DRIED (KIDNEY, PINTO, LIMA, SOY AND BLACK-EYED PEAS) Wash, pick over and discard discolored beans. Cover with boiling water, cook two minutes and remove from heat. Soak one hour or more.

Without draining, cook again, slowly, until the skins burst when you take a few on the tip of a spoon and blow on them. Correct seasoning and serve.

Many cooks like to cook dried beans with a ham hock or a piece of left-over ham, salt pork or bacon.

BEANS, GREEN AND WAX If your beans are those you've canned, do remember to cook them for about fifteen minutes before you even taste them. If they are frozen, remember they were blanched and so are somewhat pre-cooked.

With either green or wax beans you can vary them by adding sliced, sautéed mushrooms; by re-heating with ¼ cup cream and sprinkling with croutons; or by serv-·ing them Texas style. This last means you will season the beans with chili sauce to taste, then re-heat and sprinkle crumbled crisp bacon over the top.

Green beans au gratin is a handy company item, since you can put the dish together ahead of time and then put it in the oven for a half-hour at 400° just before dinner. You will want to use frozen beans for this dish, because they should be cooked in boiling water just until they are still crisp. Drain and put into a casserole in layers. Dot each layer with butter and sprinkle with salt, pepper and grated cheese. Pour light or heavy cream over all (¼ cup for each two cups of beans) and bake when ready.

BEAN SOUP, RED KIDNEY Rehydrate two pounds of dried red kidney beans. Do not drain. Without seasoning, cook in the freshening water slowly until very tender.

Sauté two cloves garlic, chopped, and two medium onions, chopped, in ¼ cup margarine or butter until the onions and garlic are pale yellow and cooked, but not brown. Puree the beans (with their liquid) in a blender or food mill. Put in a deep pan with the sautéed garlic, onion, two cups of beef bouillon and the fat. Simmer thoroughly for five or ten minutes. Serve, embellished with spoons full of yoghurt. This is enough for four hungry people.

BEAN SOUP, SENATE Once when this soup was not on the menu in the Senate dining room such a fuss was raised that it has not happened again—or, so the story goes.

Soak one pound dried great northern beans over night. The next day put on medium heat in the same water in which they were soaked, along with a ham bone, or ham hocks which have some meat on them. Add more water so that there is about a gallon of beans and all. Cook until the beans are tender and then remove the ham bone or hocks. Sauté two chopped onions in three tablespoons butter in a separate pan. Add to the soup. Correct seasoning. This serves ten to twelve people.

BEETS   We assume you know all about boiling, pickling, or making beets Harvard style. What you may not know about, unless your ancestors came from New England, is Red Flannel Hash, a dish which features beets. It is no boarding-house enigma, but has allure and snap and is solid winter fare, served piping hot with corn bread and pickles. Here's how you make it.

Fry a few slices of bacon until they're crisp. Chop about a dozen cooked beets into small pieces; mix in two or three diced boiled potatoes and two chopped onions. Cook the whole mixture in bacon fat until it's nicely brown on both sides.

A purist says that correct Red Flannel Hash is 85 per cent beets, 10 per cent potato, 3 per cent onion and 2 per cent bacon: nothing more.

Some of my best friends aren't purists though, and they grind up left-over meat to use in place of the bacon. However, the beet color and flavor predominate.

BROCCOLI (OR CAULIFLOWER) CHEESE BAKE   Start with a large bunch of cooked broccoli, or a big head of cooked cauliflower or two frozen packages of either. Place the vegetables in a shallow baking dish (10x6x2″). Blend a can of condensed mushroom or celery soup with ½ cup milk and ½ cup grated cheddar cheese. Pour this over the vegetables and top with buttered crumbs. Bake at 350° for about a half-hour, or until bubbling.

BROCCOLI AND CHEESE SOUP   This handsome melange bears little resemblance to some sad vegetarian dishes.

Use one package of frozen broccoli, or a bunch of fresh broccoli which has been separated and had the tough part of the stems removed. Cook the frozen or fresh broccoli just until tender.

Meanwhile, in another pot, melt three tablespoons butter, add three tablespoons flour and stir until smooth. Cook for a few minutes. Add a quart of milk, a little at a time, stirring constantly until smooth and the mixture is thickened. Add one cup grated cheddar cheese and cook over low heat for a few minutes until it is melted. Add the broccoli and heat all through thoroughly. This will serve four to six people.

CABBAGE   This old-time vegetable is so full of vitamin C that it should be in everyone's diet, especially through the long northern winters, but it is much maligned. Perhaps this is because too many people resent the odor of cabbage cooking, and the soggy flavor when it's improperly cooked. I tell you true, it can be odorless and perfectly delicious. Bring a pot of salted water to a rapid boil; shred the amount of cabbage desired and pop it into the water without a cover. As soon as the water returns to a full boil, start timing. After six or seven minutes, remove from the stove and drain cabbage in a colander. Butter it and serve. It will be green and slightly crunchy as are vegetables cooked Chinese style.

Don't ask me why there's no odor of cooking cabbage when the cover is left off; I only know it's so.

If you want to add a little extra to the plain cabbage, after it's cooked, re-heat in a cheese sauce with a dash of curry powder.

CABBAGE, HOT SLAW   Everybody knows how to make cole slaw, but hot slaw is good too. To make it you shred about ½ a medium cabbage. In the top of a double boiler, mix two egg yolks, ¼ cup cold water, one tablespoon butter, ¼ cup of hot vinegar and ½ teaspoon salt.

Cook over hot water, stirring constantly, until thick. Add the cabbage and re-heat.

BRUSSELS SPROUTS EN CASSEROLE   Cook sprouts just until tender, or heat through your canned ones. Season with melted butter. Put in a casserole, sprinkle with buttered crumbs and bake at 350° until crumbs are brown. For a change, you could add one cup of sliced, sautéed mushrooms to the sprouts before topping with the crumbs.

CARROTS IN HONEY   This looks and tastes so elegant that you should never explain to family or guests how very simple it is to make.

Scrub and trim really small, fresh carrots (or use those you've canned or frozen). Cook, if necessary, or heat through.

Split them from end to end, toss in plenty of strained honey mixed with some chopped mint. Arrange carrots neatly in an oven dish and cover with grated Swiss cheese. Brown under the broiler or in a 450° oven.

Try not to look smug when the compliments fly your way.

CASSEROLE OF MIXED VEGETABLES Cook vegetables especially for this dish, or use cooked left-overs. Alternate layers of well-seasoned, cooked vegetables (any kind you choose) with cooked rice, adding to each layer a bit of scraped onion or onion juice.

Pour consomme over the vegetables and dot with butter. Bake at any convenient temperature until thoroughly heated. Sprinkle with crumbled cooked bacon, or if you like, sprinkle buttered crumbs or grated cheese, or both, on top of the casserole before baking.

CELERY If you canned or froze some cooked celery, here's a great recipe in which to use it.

Put four cups cooked celery in a one-quart casserole. Stir in a five-ounce can of water chestnuts that have been sliced thin and one can condensed cream of chicken soup. For color, add one sliced pimento.

Mix lightly together and sprinkle over the casserole ½ cup soft bread crumbs, ¾ cup toasted, slivered almonds and two tablespoons of butter.

Bake at 350° for about 35 minutes. Serves six.

CORN PUDDING SOUTHERN STYLE Use rehydrated dry corn, or that which is fresh, canned or frozen. Mix two cups corn with two slightly beaten eggs. Add 1 teaspoon sugar, 1½ teaspoons melted butter, 2 cups milk, scalded, and 1 teaspoon salt. Put the mixture in a buttered baking dish and set that in a pan of warm water. Bake at 325° until firm: about 45 minutes.

OKRA This vegetable grows prolifically in warm climates and Southerners have long enjoyed using it in many ways. Some may not know about the following recipes and may enjoy using them.

If the okra has been dried, rehydrate. If the pods are small, they may be cooked whole; otherwise, the okra (whether dried, canned or frozen) should be sliced. Cook until tender and drain. Season with salt, pepper, butter and vinegar.

Another way to serve it is to stew about ½ pound of sliced okra with two cups of canned tomatoes. Season to taste.

ONION AND CHEESE CASSEROLE Have ready two cups of cooked small white onions, and one cup grated Cheddar cheese. Cut six slices of bread into quarters. Put bread, onions and cheese in layers in a buttered casserole.

Mix four slightly beaten eggs with two cups of milk and season with salt and pepper. Pour this over the mixture in the casserole and set the casserole in a pan of warm water. Bake at 350° about 45 minutes, or until firm. Serves six.

PARSNIPS I am certain that anyone who doesn't like parsnips has never had them after they've been left in the ground long enough to freeze. I don't know anything about the chemistry involved (parsnips have a right to *some* privacy), but something about the freezing makes them sweet and tasteful; they're too bland before. You can fry them, bake them, steam or boil them, and they'll be good. In our house we like this casserole, which is nice enough for guests, too.

Arrange cooked, sliced parsnips in a greased casserole, alternating with layers of grated Swiss cheese and buttered bread crumbs. Season with salt and pepper as you go. Add about one cup of light cream. Bake at 350° about 20 minutes, or until bubbly hot.

PEAS Frozen peas often lack character but can be treated so that they are exceptionally tasteful. Allow them to thaw enough so that they can be separated. Bring one tablespoon butter, one tablespoon minced shallots or green onions, and ½ cup chicken broth to boil. Add the peas, cover and boil slowly for five or six minutes, or until tender. Uncover and boil off any remaining liquid.

Your canned peas can be treated in much the same manner, if you like.

PEPPERS, GREEN Everyone knows how to stuff peppers or use them in salads and casseroles, so I thought you'd enjoy knowing about this unusual and perfectly delicious way to cook them.

Remove stems, seeds and ribs from three large green peppers and slice the peppers in strips. Place them in one layer in a shallow baking pan. Add one clove garlic, chopped, ½ cup slivered almonds, ¼ cup pitted black olives, cut in pieces, salt and pepper. Mix all together well. Over this sprinkle ½ cup well seasoned bread crumbs and pour over all ¼ cup olive oil. Bake, uncovered, at 350° for about 40 minutes, stirring occasionally.

POTATOES, WHITE Of course, you have baked, boiled, mashed and fried thousands of potatoes. Next time you're bored with all that, try this.

Boil medium-sized potatoes in their jackets. While still hot, peel them and roll each one in melted butter, then in grated cheese. Put under broiler until golden brown.

POTATOES, CANDIED SWEET Every housewife who has candied sweet potatoes, patiently skillet-watching, will appreciate this oven recipe which gives you a chance to think about something else while it's cooking.

Arrange six cooked, sliced sweet potatoes overlapping in a shallow, buttered oven dish. Pour on ¼ cup orange juice and one tablespoon lemon juice. Sprinkle over this ½ cup brown sugar with salt and pepper to taste. Dot with three tablespoons butter. Bake at 400° for 30 minutes, or until crisp and brown.

POTATO SALAD, HOT GERMAN Even on a hot day when all the rest of the meal is cold, this salad is refreshing. It's good in winter too, with a hot meal, or any day when you're not counting calories.

To serve four, cook two cups diced potatoes and one whole onion until potatoes are tender. In the meantime, cook three or four strips of bacon until crisp. Drain and crumble. When potatoes are done, drain them and remove the onion. Then add one teaspoon of raw onion grated, the bacon, and two tablespoons of hot bacon fat. Mix well and serve on lettuce immediately.

SAUERKRAUT, FRENCH STYLE (CHOUCROUTE) Cover about 2½ pounds of sauerkraut with water, then drain. Add a cup of hot boullion, 1½ cups of sauterne or chablis, and ¾ teaspoon black peppercorns or juniper berries. Simmer all this for about two hours. Then add ½ lb. of chunk bacon that has been cut into cubes and fried crisp, ¼ pound of pepperoni that has been sliced thin and ¼ pound Polish sausage sliced thin and halved. Simmer this mixture two more hours. Just before serving add sliced frankfurts, sliced ham, cooked spareribs, pork chops, knockwurst or any ham or sausage product that you like.

Serve with plain boiled potatoes and butter.

SAUERKRAUT SCHEE If you've made sauerkraut, it's because you like it a lot at your house, and here's another way to use it in a Russian soup.

Brown one cup chopped onion and two cloves minced garlic in three tablespoons butter or bacon fat. Transfer this to a soup kettle and add two cups canned tomatoes, cut in pieces; two stalks celery, chopped; two carrots, chopped; one small head cabbage cut in wedges; one turnip, quartered and four cups bouillon. Bring this mixture to a boil and simmer for 1½ hours. Then add one pound of sauerkraut, rinsed and squeezed dry, three tablespoons each of lemon juice and sugar, and one bay leaf. Simmer for another hour, adding some water if necessary. Correct seasoning. Serve with minced dill, parsley and sour cream in separate dishes. Serves four to six.

TOMATOES You must have used this versatile vegetable in dozens of different ways, but have you ever fried it? You can do so with either green or ripe tomatoes (a hint for fall), and I think you'll like it.

Dip tomato slices into flour seasoned with salt and pepper, and cook in butter or margarine over low heat until lightly browned on both sides.

TURNIPS After dicing and boiling turnip until tender, the following ideas may tempt you.

Mash drained, cooked turnip. Cook a minute or two longer to dry thoroughly. Season with butter, salt and pepper. For variety, fold in ¼ cup heavy cream, whipped, and season delicately with rum or sherry.

Or, you can go the gourmet route and make turnips

Bordelaise. Season diced cooked turnips with butter, salt
and pepper. Add garlic salt or a little crushed garlic if you
like. Put in a casserole and sprinkle with buttered bread
crumbs mixed with chopped parsley. Heat in the oven
at any convenient temperature until lightly browned.

VEGETABLE BAKE This should be in your repertoire of
dishes to serve for a buffet meal to guests. You will
need ½ cup each of chopped cabbage; diced carrots;
corn niblets; chopped green beans; diced okra; fresh,
frozen, or canned tomatoes; and cubed eggplant. Mix all
this together with two sliced onions, three tablespoons of
chopped parsley, one diced potato, and one cup olive oil.
Season with salt and pepper to taste and moisten slightly with water. Cover and bake at 350° for about an
hour. This will serve six to eight people.

ZUCCHINI There are as many delicious recipes for this
vegetable as there are Italians, and I'm sure you've tried
one or more of them, with lots of tomato and seasonings.
   A very simple and excellent way to handle the whole
matter is to slice the vegetable thinly, without peeling, and
put it into a colander: just one layer please. Put the colander in about an inch of boiling water in a covered kettle. It
takes just a few minutes to steam zucchini until tender.
Serve with butter, salt, and a sprinkling of grated Parme-
san cheese.

SAUCES AND OTHER TEMPTATIONS Crumbled hard-cooked
egg: Sprinkle over asparagus and other bright green
vegetables.
   Crumbled bacon: Goes well with almost any vegetable
except beets.
   Sautéed onions and/or sautéed mushrooms: Use to mix
with any vegetable. The onions and mushrooms together
are a delicious vegetable dish too.
   Butter and almond sauce: For almost all green vegetables
or rice. Sauté ¼ cup slivered almonds in ½ cup melted butter until golden brown. Stir in one tablespoon lemon
juice.
   Chive-lemon butter sauce: For artichokes, asparagus,

broccoli or Brussels sprouts. Place ½ cup butter, ¼ cup lemon juice and two tablespoons of fresh, frozen or dried minced chives in a saucepan. Cook over low heat until butter is melted.

FRUIT RECIPES

APPLES   There is at least one cookbook on the market devoted solely to apple recipes, so popular and versatile is this fruit. You will have stored some apples in one or more ways and probably want to try the following two, widely different ways of using them.

To make a very good stuffing for pork, goose, or duck combine two cups chopped tart apples; five cups soft bread cumbs; ½ cup raisins; two tablespoons melted butter; ¼ cup sugar, one tablespoon lemon juice; one teaspoon grated lemon peel; ½ teaspoon salt; ½ teaspoon cinnamon and ¼ cup apple juice. Mix well. This yields about five cups of stuffing.

I think you will enjoy this apple version of the old American recipe for Indian pudding. Combine 1/3 cup yellow corn meal with 1/3 cup cold water. Scald one quart of milk in the top of a double boiler; add corn meal mixture and stir over low heat until thickened. Cover and cook about 20 minutes. Remove from heat; stir in two cups thinly sliced apples; ½ teaspoon each of ginger, cinnamon and nutmeg; ½ cup molasses. Pour into greased 1½-quart casserole. Bake two hours at 325°. Serve warm or chilled, with cream, ice cream or hard sauce. Serves six.

BAKED FRUIT CRISP   Here's a tasty way to use your canned and/or frozen fruits. Don't let the kids see it until serving time: you may not have any left.

Place about a pound of apricot or pear halves and the same amount of sliced peaches in a one-quart casserole. Sprinkle with one tablespoon of lemon juice. Combine ½ cup brown sugar with 2 tablespoons melted butter and one cup cornflakes. Top the fruit with this mixture. Sprinkle with two tablespoons chopped nuts or flaked coconut, if desired. Bake for about 20 minutes at 400°. Serve with cream to four people.

CLAFOUTI   Paella, bouillabaisse, pizza and many other foreign peasant dishes have become well-liked in the U.S. My crystal ball tells me that clafouti (such an elegant name for a French peasant dessert) will achieve similar popularity, and deservedly so. It is one of the simplest possible desserts to make, and can be dressed up with liqueurs. I'm giving you a basic recipe as well as a variation for company meals. Fly with it, as people do in pizza variations. Try various fruit and berry combinations.

Put 1¼ cups milk, 1/3 cup granulated sugar, three eggs, 1 tablespoon vanilla, ¼ teaspoon salt and 2/3 cup sifted flour in your electric blender in the order given. Cover and blend at high speed for about one minute.

If you have no blender, work the eggs into the flour, gradually beat in the liquids, then strain the batter through a fine sieve.

Pour a ¼-inch layer of batter into an 8-inch pyrex pie plate that has been lightly greased. Set over moderate heat until a film of batter has set in the bottom of the dish. Remove from heat. Spread about three cups pitted sweet cherries over the batter and sprinkle on some sugar. Pour on the rest of the batter and smooth the surface with the back of a spoon.

Place on the middle shelf of your oven that is preheated to 350° and bake for about an hour. The clafouti is done when it has puffed and browned, and a knife plunged into the center comes out clean. Sprinkle the top of the clafouti with powdered sugar just before serving. It need not be served hot, but should still be warm. It will sink down slightly as it cools.

CLAFOUTI WITH LIQUEUR   Follow the basic recipe, but first let the cherries (or the fruit or berries of your choice) stand for about an hour in ¼ cup kirsch or cognac, and sugar. Substitute this liquid for ¼ cup of the milk called for in the recipe for batter. Also omit the sugar called for in the batter. Otherwise, proceed as in the basic recipe. Enjoy, enjoy!

DRIED FRUIT CANDY   The origin of this recipe is lost in the mists of time. It has long been used for gifts to be sent in metal tins to men in the service, or to other friends. Oh yes, you can eat it at home too.

You can play by ear with all kinds of fruits and quantities. I find a mixture of dried apricots, pitted prunes, seeded raisins, figs, pears and peaches is very good.

Mixing up the fruits as you go, put all through a food grinder. Then shape into balls and, if desired, roll in granulated sugar.

If stored with care, this candy keeps well for several weeks; although this reminds me of the time a friend was recommending a new cake recipe to me. When I asked if the cake kept well, she said "Not in *my* house."

MAINE BLUEBERRY PUDDING Maine has lots of goodies, and here's how the Mainiacs use one of them.

Cook three cups blueberries with ¾ cup sugar and ½ cup water for about ten minutes. Butter six slices bread and sprinkle them with cinnamon.

Put the bread and berries in a loaf pan in layers. Chill in refrigerator for several hours and serve with heavy cream to six people.

STRAWBERRY WHIP Now you know I wouldn't end a recipe chapter without including something about this Queen of Fruits! So, here you are.

Put in a bowl 1⅓ cups strawberries, cut in halves, one cup powdered sugar and one egg white. Beat this until stiff with a wire whisk or electric beater.

Serve on pieces of sponge cake or angel food, or pile it into a bowl and serve with a soft custard.

Raspberries may be substituted for strawberries in this recipe.

STRAWBERRY-PEACH BOWL In a bowl mix a cup of fresh, halved strawberries (or a package of frozen sliced berries, thawed), and a package of frozen peach slices, thawed (or a cup of canned, or fresh peach slices). Serve in individual dishes topped with whipped or sour cream.

Frozen or fresh raspberries may be substituted for strawberries in this recipe.

BIBLIOGRAPHY

Allen, E. J., Extension Horticulturist, University of Arkansas. Personal communication. Sept. 1971.

Auburn University, Alabama. Co-op. Extension Service. Circular HE-19, Wise Methods of Canning Vegetables, 1967.

Ball Corporation, Ball Blue Book. Muncie, Indiana, 1966.

Banadyga, A. A., Horticulturist, Extension Service, No. Carolina State University. Personal communication. Sept. 1971.

Burnham, Milo, Extension Horticulturist. Co-op Extension Service, Mississippi State University. Personal communication. Sept. 1971.

Foster, Gertrude, Herbs for Every Garden. E. P. Dutton & Co., New York, 1966.

Frickson, Charlotte, The Freezer Cookbook. Chilton Book Co., New York, Philadelphia, London. 1968.

Gustafson, A. F., E. V. Hardenburg, E. Y. Smith, Jeannette McCay, Land for the Family. Comstock Publishing Co., Ithaca, N.Y. 1947.

Heid, J. L., M. A. Joslyn, Fundamentals of Food Processing Operations. Avi Publishing Co., Westport, Conn. 1967.

Heriteau, Jacqueline, The How to Grow and Cook it Book of Vegetables, Herbs, Fruits and Nuts. Hawthorn Books, Inc., New York. 1970.

Holmes, A. D. Storage Life of Mature and Immature Butternut Squashes. American Dietetic Assoc. Journal, vol. 29, 1953.

Kirtland, Helen, Mgr. Consumers Institute, General Electric Co. Personal communication, August, 1971.

Levinson, L. L., The Complete Book of Pickles and Relishes. Hawthorn Books, Inc., New York, 1965.

Light, R. G., Prof. Agricultural Engineering, University of Massachusetts. Personal communication, November, 1971.

Louisiana Co-op. Extension Service. Home Canning of Fruits and Vegetables, 1969.

Martineau, Stanley, Payson, Arizona. Personal communication, January, 1972.

Meyer, Hazel, The Complete Book of Home Freezing. J. B. Lippincott, New York, 1964.

Nearing, Helen and Scott, Living the Good Life. Schocken Books, New York, 1970.

Newsom, D. W., Dept. of Horticulture, Louisiana State University. Personal communication, September, 1971.

Robinson, Ed and Carolyn, Have-More Plan. Garden Way Publishing Co., Charlotte, Vt., 1943. (Out of print).

Robinson, Carolyn, Brooksville, Maine. Personal communication, October, 1971.

Rodale and Staff, Encyclopedia of Organic Gardening. Rodale Books, Emmaus, Pa., 1959.

Rodale and Staff, How to Grow Vegetables and Fruits by the Organic Method. Rodale Books, Emmaus, Pa., 1961.

Roth, June, The Freeze and Please Home Cookbook. Frederick Fell Inc., New York, 1963.

Rowley, Charles, Pres. Arctic Sauna Corp. Personal communication, July, 1971.

Seranne, Ann, The Complete Book of Home Preserving. Doubleday and Co., Inc., Garden City, N.Y., 1955.

U.S.D.A., Yearbook of Agriculture, Farmer's World, 1964. Supt. of Documents, Washington, D.C.

U.S.D.A., Home and Garden Bulletin No. 10, Home Freezing of Fruits and Vegetables, 1970. Supt. of Documents, Washington, D.C.

U.S.D.A., Bulletin No. 119, Storing Vegetables and Fruits in Basements, Cellars, Outbuildings and Pits, 1967. Supt. of Documents, Washington, D.C.

U.S.D.A., Home and Garden Bulletin No. 8, Home Canning of Fruits and Vegetables, 1969. Supt. of Documents, Washington, D.C.

Wilson, Anna, Extension Nutritionist, University of Vermont, Freezing Storage Well Used. Undated.

Wilson, Anna, Extension Nutritionist, University of Vermont, Freezing Handbook. Undated.

Wise Garden Encyclopedia, Grosset and Dunlap, New York, 1970.

Wright, Alice, Asst. Nutritionist, Extension Service, University of Vermont. Personal communication, August, 1971.

INDEX

Advantages of
canning, 61
drying, 34
freezing, 89

Apples
canning of, 77
common storage of, 30
varieties for, 30
drying of, 46
freezing of, 128, 129
pudding recipe, 146
stuffing recipe, 146

Apricots
drying of, 46
freezing of, 129, 130

Artichokes, freezing of, 108

Ascorbic-citric acid, use of, 77, 124, 125

Asparagus
canning of, 81
freezing of, 108, 109
recipe for, 136

Barrels for outdoor storage, 15, 22

Basic rules for,
canning, 67, 68
common storage, indoor, 20, 21
common storage, outdoor, 8, 9
curing and salting, 53
drying, 51
freezing, 95, 96

Beans, butter, canning of, 82
Boston baked recipe, 136, 137
dried, canning of, 81
recipe for, 137
green, canning of, 82
casserole of, 137, 138
Lima, canning of, 82
freezing of, 109, 110
snap, canning of, 82
drying of, 46
freezing of, 110
weak brining of, 59, 60
soy, canning of, 82
wax, canning of, 82
casserole of, 137, 138
freezing of, 110

Beets
canning of, 82, 83
common storage of, 25
drying of, 46
greens, freezing of, 111
red flannel hash recipe, 139
weak brining of, 59, 60

Blackberries
canning of, 78
freezing of, 134

Blanching
for drying, 36
for freezing, 99-103

Blueberries
canning of, 78
freezing of, 134
pudding recipe, 148

Botulism, 69

Broccoli
canning of, 83
cheese bake recipe, 139
cheese soup recipe, 139
freezing of, 111, 112

Brussels sprouts,
canning of, 83
casserole of, 140
freezing of, 112
ground storage of, 19

Cabbage
drying of, 46
freezing of, 112, 113
ground storage of, 18, 19
hot slaw recipe, 140
sauerkraut, 53-56

Canning
apples, 77
sauce, 77
ascorbic-citric acid, 77
asparagus, 81
basic rules for, 67, 68
beans,
butter and Lima, 82
dried, 81
green, snap and wax, 82
soy, 82
beets, 82, 83
berries, 78
botulism in, 69
broccoli, 83
Brussels sprouts, 83
carrots, 83
cauliflower, 83, 84
celery, 84
celery and tomatoes, 84
cherries, 78, 79
cold pack method in, 67, 68
corn,
cream style, 85
whole kernel, 84, 85
enzymatic action in vegetables and fruits, 61, 62
equipment for, 63-67
grapefruit, 79
hot pack method in, 67, 68
lids for, 65
methods of, 67, 68
mixed vegetables, 85, 86
mushrooms, 86
peaches, 79, 80
pears, 80
peas, black-eyed, 86, 87
green, 87
potatoes, sweet, 87
rhubarb, 80, 81
seals, 75
spoilage in foods, 68, 69
squash summer, 88
steam-pressure canner for, 63
canning with, 74
care of, 66
storage of canned foods, 75, 76
strawberries, 78
succotash, 87, 88
syrups for, 77
tables
altitude chart, 73
food planning guide, 62
jar estimating, 64
what's the cause? 70-72
test for quality in, 88
tomatoes,
juice, 76
salad, 76
warnings about, 68, 69
water-bath canner, 66
canning with, 73-75

Carrots
canning of, 83
common storage of, 25
drying of, 46
freezing of, 113
in honey, recipe, 140, 141
weak brining of, 59

Cartons, outdoor storage, 15

Case hardening (in drying), 45

Casseroles
bean, 137, 138
broccoli cheese bake, 139
Brussels sprouts, 140
mixed vegetables, 141
onion and cheese, 142
parsnips and cheese, 142

Cauliflower
canning of, 83, 84
freezing of, 113, 114
ground storage of, 19
weak brining of, 59, 60

Celery
basement, 18
canning, 84
casserole, 141
drying, 46
freezing, 114
ground storage, 16-18
and tomatoes, canning, 84

Cherries
canning of, 78, 79
drying of, 46
freezing of, 130

Chinese cabbage, outdoor storage of, 16

Citrus fruits
common storage, indoor, 31
grapefruit, canning of, 79
oranges, freezing of, 132

Clafouti, recipe for, 147

Cleaning for outdoor storage, 9

Climate
for drying, 38
for outdoor storage, 11

Cold pack method, canning, 67, 68

Collard greens, freezing of, 114

Common storage (see also Root cellar)
apples, varieties for, 30
methods of, 31
citrus fruits, 31
containers for, 22, 23
facilities for, 23, 24
general rules for, 20, 21
humidity for, 22
miscellaneous root crops for,
harvesting of, 25
storing of, 25
onions
harvesting of, 25
storing of, 25
peppers, green,
harvesting of, 25
storing of, 26
peppers, hot,
harvesting of, 26
storing of, 26
potatoes, harvesting of, 26
potatoes, early
storing of, 26, 27
potatoes, late
harvesting of, 27
storing of, 27
potatoes, sweet
harvesting of, 27
curing and storing of, 27
pumpkins and squashes
harvesting of, 27
curing and storing of, 28
stairwells for, 23
temperature and ventilation for, 21, 22
tomatoes
harvesting of, 28, 29
storing of, 29

Common storage, outdoor
(see also Ground storage)
barrels for, 15, 22
basic rules for, 8, 9
cartons for, 15
cleaning for, 9
climate for, 12
mound for, 12
directions for making, 12, 13
packing for, 11
pit for, 13, 14
directions for making, 14, 15
tile for, 15

Conditioning of dried foods, 45, 47

Containers
for canning, 64
for common storage, 22, 23
for dried foods, 47

Corn
cream style, canning of, 85
freezing of, 116, 117
drying of, 46
pudding recipe, 141
whole kernel, canning of, 84, 85
freezing of, 117

Crabapples, freezing of, 130

Cranberries, freezing of, 131

Curing and salting
fermentation in, 52
general directions for, 53
history of, 52
lettuce kraut, 58
nutritive values in, 52
salt for, 52
sauer beans, cauliflower, green tomatoes, 59
sauerkraut, 53-57
canning of, 56, 57
directions for making, 55, 56
equipment for making, 54
Florida quick method, 57
spoilage, causes of, 57, 58
turnip kraut (sauerruben), 58
weak brining, 59, 60

Disadvantages, of drying, 34, 35

Dried fruit candy, recipe, 147, 148

Drying
advantages of, 34
blanching for, 36
case hardening in, 45
conditioning in, 47
containers for, 47
disadvantages of, 34, 35
herbs, 48
crushing of, 50
harvesting of, 49
paper bag drying of, 49, 50
screen drying of, 49
storage of, 49
history of, 32
preparing individual products (Table 3), 46
methods of, 38, 39, 44, 45
nutritive values in, 33, 34
oven drying, 44
electricity costs of, 44
pre-cooking for, 36
plans for driers, 40-44
preparation of produce for, 35, 36
principles of, 33
rehydration of dried foods, 47, 48
selection of produce for, 35
sulfuring in, 36, 37
substitutes for, 38
sun-drying, 38
tests for doneness in, 45

Dry sugar pack, 126

Endive, ground storage of, 18

Enzymatic action, 36, 61, 62, 100

Equipment for
canning, 63-67
curing and salting, 54
drying, 40-44
freezing, 94

Fermentation, 52

Figs,
drying of, 46

Food planning guide, 62

Freezer, maintenance
costs for, 92-94
power failure, 103-105
purchasing of, 89, 90
types of, 90-93

Freezing
basic rules for, 95, 96
blanching for, 99-103
boiling, 102, 103
steaming, 102
equipment for, 94
fruits and berries, 123, 124
apples, 128, 129
apricots, 129, 130
ascorbic-citric acid, use of, 124, 125
blackberries, 134
blueberries, 134
cherries, sour, 130
sweet 130
crabapples, 130
cranberries, 131
dry sugar pack for, 126
fruit juices, 131, 132

grapefruit, 132
oranges, 132
packaging of, 124
peaches, 132, 133
preparation of, 124
raspberries, 134, 135
rhubarb, 133
storage time of, 128
strawberries, 135
syrups for, 127, 128
syrup pack for, 127
unsweetened dry pack for, 125, 126
unsweetened wet pack for, 126
thawed foods in, 105
of vegetables, 108
artichokes, 108
asparagus, 108, 109
beans, Lima, snap or wax, 109, 110
soy, 110
beets, 110, 111
greens, 111
broccoli, 111, 112
Brussels sprouts, 112
cabbage, 112, 113
carrots, 113
cauliflower, 113, 114
celery, 114
collard greens, 114
corn, 115-117
cream style, 116, 117
whole kernel, 117
herbs, 117, 118
kale, 118
mustard greens, 118
okra, 118
peas, 119
peppers, green, 119, 120
potatoes, sweet, 120
potatoes, white stuffed, 121
pumpkin, 121
spinach, 121
squash, summer, 122
squash, winter, 122
Swiss chard, 122
tomatoes, 122, 123
yield from fresh produce, Table 8, 106, 107
Fruits and berries,
canning of, 77-81
freezing of, 123-128
Grapefruit, canning of, 79
freezing of, 132

Ground storage
Brussels sprouts, 19
cabbage, 18, 19
cauliflower, 18, 19
celery, 16-18
Chinese cabbage, 16-18
endive, 18
root crops, 25

Herbs
crushing of, 50
drying of, 48-51
freezing of, 117, 118
harvesting of, 49
mixtures to dry or freeze
bouquet garni, 51
fines herbes, 117, 118
fish flavoring, 51
for spaghetti sauce, 51
for tossed salads, 51
for poultry stuffing, 51
ravigote, 51
stewing herbs, 51

History of curing and salting, 52
of drying, 32
Hot pack for canning, 68
Kale,
freezing of, 118
weak brining of, 59, 60
Kraut (see lettuce kraut, sauerkraut and turnip kraut)
Lettuce kraut, 58
Lids, for canning, 65
Methods, of canning, 67, 68
warnings, 68, 69
of drying, 38, 39

Mixed vegetables, canning of, 85, 86
Mushrooms, canning of, 86
Mustard greens, freezing of, 118
Nutritive values retained in
canning, 61
common storage, 16
curing and salting, 52
drying, 33, 34
freezing, 100
Okra, freezing of, 118
recipe for, 141, 142
Onions
harvesting and storing of, 25
casserole recipe, 142
drying of, 46
Oranges, freezing of, 132
Outdoor mounds, plans for, 12, 13
Outdoor pit, plan for, 13-15
Oven drying, 39
electricity cost of, 39
Packaging, for freezing, 96-99
Packing for outdoor storage, 11
Parsnips, casserole recipe, 142
drying of, 46
Peaches,
canning of, 79, 80
drying of, 46
freezing of, 132, 133
Pears, canning of, 80
common storage of, 31
varieties for, 31
when to pick, 31
drying of, 46
Peas, black-eyed, canning of, 86, 87
Peas, green, canning of, 87
drying of, 46
freezing of, 119
Peppers, green
harvesting and storing for, 25, 26
drying of, 46
freezing of, 119, 120
recipe for, 142, 143
Peppers, hot
drying and storage of, 26
Plans for
basement storage room, 23, 24
driers, 40-44
outdoor mound, 12, 13
outdoor pit, 13-15
Potatoes, sweet
canning of, 87
candied, recipe for, 143
harvesting and curing for, 27
freezing of, 120
Potatoes, white,
early, 26
common storage of, 27
late, 27
common storage of, 27
freezing of, 121
recipes, 143
Pre-cooking, for drying, 36
Pumpkins,
harvesting and curing of, 27, 28
storing of, 28
drying of, 46
freezing of, 121
Raspberries, canning of, 78
freezing of, 134, 135
Recipes,
apple Indian pudding, 146
apple stuffing, 146
asparagus, 136
baked fruit crisp, 146
beans, Boston baked, 136, 137
dried, all kinds, 137
green and wax casserole, 137, 138
soups, 138
broccoli cheese bake, 139

broccoli and cheese soup, 139
Brussels sprouts casserole, 140
cabbage, 140
hot slaw, 140
carrots in honey, 140, 141
casserole mixed vegetables, 141
celery casserole, 141
clafouti, 147
corn pudding, 141
dried fruit candy, 147, 148
Maine blueberry pudding, 148
okra, 141, 142
onion and cheese casserole, 142
parsnip casserole, 142
peas, 142
peppers, roasted, 142, 143
potatoes, broiled, 143
potatoes, candied sweet, 143
potato salad, hot German, 143
red flannel hash, 139
sauces and other temptations, 145, 146
sauerkraut, French style, 143, 144
sauerkraut schee, 144
strawberry whip, 148
strawberry-peach bowl, 148
tomatoes, sautéed, 144
turnip, 144, 145
vegetable bake, 145
zucchini, 145
Rehydration, dried foods, 47, 48
Rhubarb, canning of, 80, 81
freezing of, 133
Root cellar
apples, 30, 31
celery, 18
containers for, 15
humidity of, 22
miscellaneous root crops, 25
onions, 25
potatoes, 26, 27
pumpkins and squashes, 27, 28
temperature and ventilation of, 21, 22
tomatoes, 28, 29
Rutabagas, common storage of, 25
weak brining of, 59, 60
Salt, "pure" or canning, 53, 66
Sauces and other temptations, 145, 146
Sauer beans, cauliflower and green tomatoes, 59, 60
Sauna, 24
Sauerkraut, 53-57
canning of, 56, 57
directions for making, 55, 56
equipment for making, 54
Florida quick method, 57
recipes, 143, 144
spoilage, causes of, 57, 58
Spinach, drying of, 46
freezing of, 121
Spoilage, causes of,
in canned foods, 70-72
in kraut, 57, 58
Squash
harvesting and curing for, 27
storing, 28
drying of, 46
summer, canning of, 88
freezing of, 122
winter, freezing of, 122
Steam-pressure canner, 63
care of, 66
way to use, 74

Storage methods,
canning, 4, 5
fruits and vegetables for, 2
nutritive values retained in, 4
common storage, 1, 3
fruits and vegetables for, 2
nutritive values retained in, 3
curing and salting, 4
nutritive values retained in, 4
vegetables for, 2
drying, 3, 4
fruits and vegetables for, 2
nutritive values retained in, 3
freezing, 5
fruits and vegetables for, 2
nutritive values retained in, 5
general rules, all methods, 5, 6
Strawberries, canning of, 78
freezing of, 135
recipes for, 148
Succotash, canning of, 87, 88
Sulfuring, 36, 37
substitutes for, 38
Sun-drying, 38
Swiss chard, freezing of, 122
Syrups, fruit canning, 77
fruit freezing, 127, 128
Syrup pack, 127
Tables
altitude chart, 73
common storage information, 10
food planning guide, 62
general storage information 2
how to prepare and dry vegetables and fruits, 46
jar estimating, 64
what's the cause? 70-72
yield of frozen produce from fresh, 106, 107
Tests for
doneness in drying, 45
seals of canned foods, 75
Thawed foods, 105
Tile storage, 15
Tomatoes,
canning of, 76
juice, 76
salad tomatoes, 76
harvesting and storing for, 28, 29
freezing of, 122, 123
recipe for, 144
Turnip
common storage of, 25
drying of, 46
recipes for, 144, 145
sauerruben, 58
weak brining of, 59, 60
Unsweetened dry pack, 125
wet pack, 126
Water-bath canner, 66
way to use, 72-74
Weak brining, 59
directions for, 60
Yield from fresh produce
frozen, 106, 107
canned, 62